Faith
Prints

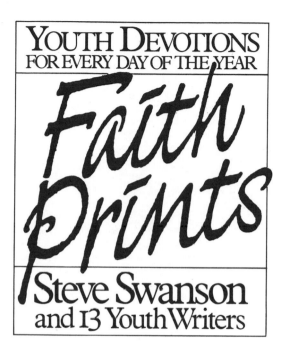

YOUTH DEVOTIONS
FOR EVERY DAY OF THE YEAR

Faith prints

Steve Swanson
and 13 Youth Writers

AUGSBURG Publishing House • Minneapolis

FAITH PRINTS
Youth Devotions for Every Day of the Year

Scripture quotations unless otherwise noted are from the Holy Bible: New
International Version. Copyright 1978 by the New York International
Bible Society. Used by permission of Zondervan Bible Publishers.

Scripture quotations marked TEV are from the Good News Bible, Today's
English Version, copyright 1966, 1971, 1976 by American Bible Society.
Used by permission.

Photos: Mimi Forsyth, 23, 144; Gene Plaisted, 48; Jean-Claude Lejeune,
65, 119, 198; Ron Meyer, 91; Elizabeth Wood, 169; Carita Parker, 220.

Library of Congress Cataloging-in-Publication Data

Swanson, Stephen O.
  FAITH PRINTS.

  1. Youth—Prayer-books and devotions—English.
2. Devotional calendars.   I. Title.
BV4850.S94   1985   242'.2   85-13466
ISBN 0-8066-2178-8

Manufactured in the U.S.A.   APH 10-2189

            6   7   8   9   0   1   2   3   4   5   6   7   8   9

About This Book

Youth speaking to youth speaking to God—that is what this devotional book is about. The devotions are meant to help young people as they pray and meditate on their life in faith. The difference is that most of the devotions are written by youth writers, ages 14 to 20. They know the struggles young people face, because they are living them. They can express the joys of Christian life in the language and images of youth because they are youth.

The writers were selected through a nationwide competition sponsored by the Luther League of the American Lutheran Church. Thirteen youth writers were selected from many fine entries, and these were given further training at a conference funded by American Lutheran Church Women.

Faith Prints contains a year's worth of devotions, organized by weeks. Each week is based on a different passage from the Bible, from which the writer draws several devotional ideas. The week begins with a Sunday devotion written by Steve Swanson—author, college professor, and adviser to the youth writers.

While the book may be begun at any time in the year, the texts were chosen to coordinate with the church year that is followed by many Christian denominations, which begins about the first of December. The wide variety of biblical texts brings out many different aspects of Christian life. If you want to begin the book in the middle of the year, yet follow the themes, simply figure out which week of the calendar year you are in, and add four.

Let us introduce the youth writers to you.

5

Jay A. Bates. High-school senior from Tacoma, Washington. Exuberant owner of a large hat collection.

Elaine Marion Becker. High-school senior from Alden, New York. Always ready with a smile and a hug.

Sue Debner. High-school junior from Greene, Iowa. Puts her Christian concern into action through work with mentally retarded children.

Pamela A. Fletcher. College sophomore from Sierra Vista, Arizona. Wrestles with faith and life, is looking forward to working with Christians overseas.

Karleen Kos. College junior from Point Lookout, Missouri. Keen insight and a common-sense voice from the Ozarks.

Kathryn Larmore. College freshman from Hales Corners, Wisconsin. Turned a lost suitcase into a contest-winning devotion.

T. Lea Maul. High-school sophomore from Baltimore, Maryland. Plays a mean game of volleyball.

Thien Huu Pham. College sophomore from San Diego, California. Combines artistic and scientific talents with a wide variety of experiences.

Paul J. Reinschmidt. High-school freshman from Rochester, Minnesota. Interested in a broad range of intellectual pursuits.

Janell Joan Sill. Secretary from Brownton, Minnesota. A life guided by a personal faith that shows in her writing.

Jill Sundby. College junior from Rapid City, South Dakota. Quiet world traveler with active interests in writing and photography.

Dan Wahl. College freshman from Revere, Minnesota. Expresses many fresh insights through prose and poetry.

Andrew Wold. High-school freshman from Peru, Illinois. Exploring interests in writing and music.

Those are the people. Now, let their writing speak to you as you speak to God.

Week 1   Psalm 96
New Year's Resolution (Sunday)

Dave was up early on New Year's Day, early, that is, for a holiday. At 8:15 he was singing away in the kitchen, frying eggs and getting ready to go skiing with the youth group.

"Do you have to sing?" his mother asked, her hands over her ears. Her slippers looked like two cottontail rabbits playing underneath the fringe of her bathrobe. She was kidding about his singing, of course, but Dave felt there was a kind of envy in it, a deep wish for some of his joy. He had a happiness that his mom and dad hadn't found yet. It came out in singing.

Dave wondered if his name had anything to do with the way he liked to sing. King David wrote songs and played the harp, and young David sang for old Saul when Saul had one of his spells.

Dave wished he could sing his folks into joy. He wished he could sing the songs of his faith and somehow transfer some of his faith to his parents. He knew their life would be better if they came to believe, and if they joined the church, and if they put their lives in the hands of God. A lot of "ifs."

Dave wanted to make a New Year's resolution about that: "This year I resolve to get my parents going in church." But how could a kid get his parents to do anything? Dave's friend Andy couldn't even keep his parents from getting divorced.

I will keep singing, though, Dave thought to himself. *And around home I'll sing the familiar hymns, the ones mom and dad know from the old days. Maybe that will get us talking about religion sometimes.*

That became Dave's New Year's resolution. He would sing to the Lord the *old* songs.   SS

New Song (Monday)

"Sing to the Lord a new song" (Ps. 96:1).

I was singing with the congregation in church and feeling pretty good about it. My voice rang out clearly, matching the organ note for note. The second verse started, but I didn't. A sour note from the pew behind me stopped me short. *He just ruined the whole hymn,* I thought to myself. After a while, I started singing again, and soon the service was over.

Then I started thinking, *This is ridiculous. There I was, trying to praise God with my voice and forgetting the song of love and forgiveness. I should be singing a new song, composed of deeds, not just words.* I didn't have to wait until next Sunday to sing this new song. I could start now, today!   DW

Mustang Blues (Tuesday)

"For all the gods of the nations are idols" (Ps. 96:5).

He knelt before the fender and caressed it with his wax rag, then petted it. His mother walked in. "What are you doing?" she asked.

"Just waxing my car, mom," he said with obvious pride.

"Oh, Kirby, I don't know what we're going to do with you," she sighed. "Doesn't anything else matter to you besides your car? You waxed it two days ago!"

"Nothing compares to my Ford." Kirby said with determination.

His mom went over in her mind how she could explain to Kirby that the god he had was nothing compared to the real God he would feel better having. *Your god can run out of gas, Kirb,* she thought.   DW

Gift of Dawn (Wednesday)

"Bring an offering, and come into his courts" (Ps. 96:8).

Dawn's older brother was an artist. Her baby brother was good at getting attention for his *goo*-ings and *gaa*-ings. *But I'm not good at anything,* she decided.

Dawn just hadn't yet realized her gifts, the things she was good at. The offering you can give to God is the thing you do well. It doesn't matter if you don't know what you do well—that will come with time. God admires and accepts anything you have to offer, even if you don't know what it is yourself. Give of yourself and give freely. Bring an offering, and come into his courts!

DW

A Planned Passing (Thursday)

"He will judge the world in righteousness" (Ps. 96:13).

Jim sat on the fire escape and stared at the traffic below. Pedestrians walked over the place on the sidewalk where his brother had plummeted from the iron bar Jim balanced on. "No one cares," he murmured. "God doesn't care." He was sick of the reassurances—"It's God's will that he be taken, Jim." He snapped his head skyward and screamed, "Why?"

The Bible talks a lot about suffering, and about people who asked hard questions about God. But it also says that God became a person in Jesus. God knows what it's like to suffer and die, and even Jesus asked, "Why?"

DW

Delivery Man (Friday)

"Declare his glory among the nations" (Ps. 96:3).

David Nelson approached the man seated at the desk. "Hello, Mr. Trent. I'm from the Church of—"

The man cut him short. "I'm busy."

"But Mr. Trent, we heard that you just got this job and that you're new in town, and I thought—"

"I happen to work for a living. Now if you'll excuse me." The man returned to his work.

Outside the office building, David sat down on the cold concrete. He remembered that verse, "Declare his glory." David didn't like some of the reactions he got when he *did* declare God's glory. But he tried to be personal about it, and he would let God worry about the results.   DW

Dream Song (Saturday)

"Let the fields be jubilant, and everything in them" (Ps. 96:12).

Caroline nestled into her bed. Soon she was dreaming, and in her dream she leaned on her windowsill to find out what the noise in her garden was all about. The tomatoes were tittering, and the cucumbers burst into song. She called to her sister, "I can't believe my ears! We have veggies praising God!"

"That's funny," her sister replied. "They usually just babble on about the stock market."

"Yeah!" she said.

Caroline awoke, and all the rest of the day she sang the song of her dreams.   DW

Week 2   Matthew 2
Epiphany Can Mean Insight (Sunday)

Angie heard the pastor read the Epiphany text and thought of Jan. Mary and Joseph were trying to protect their baby from Herod, bloody Herod the tyrant. It took the Wise Men and an angel dream to hustle them off into Egypt. Jan was hiding her baby too. Only Jan had had no angel dreams, nor Wise Men either. Jan so far had nobody—not even Bryan, the rat. Got her pregnant, then threw her away like trash.

Angie had told him off. "It's your baby too," she had screamed, her nose a foot away from his. "How can you treat Jan like this?"

"Butt out," Bryan said. "It's none of your business." He turned and walked away.

"It *is* my business," Angie shouted at his back. "She's my friend."

So now, a month later, Angie wanted to know what a friend should do. Jan can't run away to Egypt. Her baby isn't destined to be God. This isn't the Holy Spirit's work. It isn't a miracle. It has been nightmare all the way—weakness and mistakes and fear and frustration—and Jan carrying it all. Now she's putting off a decison.

When Angie first heard about the baby, she advised Jan to tell her parents. Jan wouldn't. "They care too much about what people think. They'll tell me to have an abortion." Then after a long pause, "I won't do that."

Angie wanted to help Jan do what was right. *She needs more help than I can give,* she thought. *I'm going to catch the pastor after church. I'll tell him how his sermon made me think of Jan and how. . .*   SS

Awaken to Worship (Monday)

"We. . . have come to worship him" (Matt. 2:2).

I sleepily shut off my noisy alarm. Yesterday had been a struggle, and I felt exhausted. Pulling the covers over my head, I vowed to sleep in. Yet when mom called that it was time for church, I jumped into my church clothes and rushed downstairs.

All the way to church I quizzed myself. Why did I feel so obligated to go to church? So I wouldn't disappoint my parents? To make a good impression on my friends? Or did I really want to worship my Lord?

I recalled the simple confirmation definition for worship: worth-ship, Jesus is my king. He is worth all my love and devotion. His name is worthy of all honor and praise. I was glad I had finally awakened to worship my king.   JJS

A Ruler for God's People (Tuesday)

". . . a ruler who will be the shepherd of my people. . . " (Matt. 2:6).

"Janell, would you please stop those big boys from picking on my little brother?" Heidi begged me. We were on our way home on the school bus, and a couple of high school boys were bringing tears to the eyes of my little neighbor boy, Chad.

I went back and told the boys to pick on someone their own size and sent Chad to sit up front. Heidi was grateful.

No matter who you are, there is always someone who admires you and looks to you for help. As a "ruler" of those younger than I and an influence on my teenage friends, I try to set a good example. I look to the perfect ruler for help, that I may lead others in God's ways.   JJS

Searching for the Ultimate (Wednesday)

"Go and make a careful search. . . " (Matt. 2:8).

After ransacking my room three times I finally found my car keys in a jacket pocket. Another frantic search was over.

It seems that I'm always looking for something. My search is not just for objects I have misplaced. I keep looking for new and more exciting experiences, ideas, and pleasures in life. I long to discover that which will give me a more meaningful life.

How thankful I am that Jesus came to this earth and revealed his wonderful salvation to us. Without his help I would be searching for a lifetime and still not discover the ultimate source of life and joy in my God. I was lost, but he sought and found me.   JJS

Gifts for the King (Thursday)

"Then they opened their treasures and presented him with gifts of gold and of incense and of myrrh" (Matt. 2:11).

The offering plate was passed, and I put in my usual dollar. I could have given a little more, but the stereo system I have my eye on will be on sale soon.

I'm hooked on quality stereos. Since I received my first stereo when I was nine, I have purchased two new systems, and now I am thinking of buying another. Technology changes so fast that it's hard on my budget to keep up with it all.

I wonder how the church keeps up with inflation if everyone keeps giving the same amount year after year as I have been doing. Jesus gave his very best to me. Do I dare give him any less in return?   JJS

Bright Side of a Dark Beginning (Friday)

"Get up,. . . take the child and his mother, and escape to Egypt" (Matt. 2:13).

I love the Christmas season with its news of peace on earth and good will to men. Yet so quickly we get away from it. The daily news speaks about war and crime, accidents and death. What a dark beginning to a new year!

Yet there is a bright side. Jealous Herod plotted to kill the newborn king. The holy family had to sneak off into the night like common fugitives. But Herod did not succeed. God's chosen one still went on to win the victory of our salvation.

Our Christian beliefs and values may often be rejected by the world, but we are still God's chosen people. Though we suffer setbacks and defeats, our final victory is assured, for God is with us.   JJS

Dreaming about Angels (Saturday)

". . . angel of the Lord appeared in a dream to Joseph. . . " (Matt. 2:19).

Have you ever seen an angel? I haven't, but I keep hoping that I'll get my chance someday. I have a lot of questions I'd like to ask angels about their work, about heaven, and about my own future life.

As Joseph remained open to God's leading, an angel appeared to him in a dream on at least three occasions. All three times Joseph received news that influenced the safety and happiness of his family.

I'm sure that God will also speak to us again this year, if not through an angel, then certainly through his inspired Word which is available to us every day of our lives. God will reveal his plans for our lives and direct us safely in his ways.   JJS

Week 3   1 Samuel 3:1-21

Those Who Help Us Hear God's Call (Sunday)

We wonder how many times God would have called Samuel if Eli hadn't been around. Maybe it's harder when you're young. Samuel was just a boy. What did he know of voices in his sleep, of the voice of the Lord calling him to respond, not only with his ears, but with his mind and soul and heart—indeed, with his whole life?

You ever had the feeling God was calling you? Maybe the call seemed vague, like a dream, a haunting feeling, like a soft voice in the night. The voice was soft enough so you didn't explode out of bed and hit the floor running, but it was insistent enough so that you knew God wanted you to *do* something—or to *be* something.

Samuel went to Eli, to someone he trusted, someone he loved, someone older in the Lord. At first, even Eli didn't recognize what was happening to Samuel. After all, Samuel was just a boy. Who would have expected it?

When you have a spiritual concern, when the voices are troubling you, be sure you keep going to your Eli until he listens, until he gives you good advice.

And what was Eli's advice to Samuel? "Be receptive," he said. Eli told Samuel to say this: "Speak, Lord, for your servant is listening." That receptivity, that openness to the message of God is all-important. The message can come in many ways, *but it will come.* It may come through the Bible—read it. It may come through prayer—practice it. It may come through the church—attend it. It may come through God's people—hear and heed them.   SS

Don't Procrastinate (Monday)

"Then the Lord called Samuel" (1 Sam. 3:4).

Every once in a while, when I'm contentedly doing something, I hear one of my parents call out, "Jay Alan, will you come here, please?" I know right away that I am either in trouble or some kind of work needs to be done. Being the typical teenage procrastinator, I take as much time to respond as I can without getting yelled at.

When God calls us, many of us are tempted to procrastinate. But as Christians we won't want to take our time to carry out God's will. It is an honor that we won't want to pass up.   JAB

Listen (Tuesday)

"Speak, for your servant is listening" (1 Sam. 3:10).

Listen
to God.
God has spoken.
And when God speaks,
he wants your full attention.
Listen and hear God's word thunder
above the heavens and earth.
God's message is clear,
and very simple
To hear.
Listen!   JAB

Don't Be Afraid to Be Afraid (Wednesday)

"He was afraid to tell Eli the vision" (1 Sam. 3:15).

I get nervous when I hear someone say "hypodermic needle." Fear is something that lives in us all. Even the "greatest" of all our great-grandparents, Adam and Eve, were afraid to face God, because they were naked.

Many of us, when we are afraid, hold it to ourselves and don't tell anyone, even God. Yet that is the opposite of what we should do. Whenever fear overtakes us, whether it be on a rickety bridge or during a thunderstorm, we should talk to God, the best comforter around.

"When I am afraid, I will trust in you" (Ps. 56:3).

JAB

It Takes More than Works (Thursday)

"The guilt of Eli's house will never be atoned for by sacrifice or offering" (1 Sam. 3:14).

At one time or another, all of us try to "bargain" with God. I don't know how many times I have said, "Lord, if you do this for me, I promise never to sin again." Or have you ever wanted to earn your way to being with God in heaven by being extra good? I think we all are guilty of doing that too.

No matter how many different ways we try to please God, there is only one true way: by faith in Jesus Christ. God loves us so much that we don't need to do special things to impress him. Our love and total devotion is all God asks. "For it is by grace you have been saved, through faith" (Eph. 2:8).

JAB

The Lord Knows What's Best (Friday)

"He is the Lord; let him do what is good in his eyes" (1 Sam. 3:18).

After being invited out by one of my friends, I ask my mom, "Can I go see a movie tonight?" Expecting a yes, I hear a "No, it would be best if you stayed home." After arguing for a bit, I go to my room and pout. *She doesn't know what's best for me,* I say to myself. Yet, as much as I hate to admit it, she is probably right.

Sometimes, when we ask God for something, the answer is no. As much as we may not believe it, God loves us and wants us to have the very best, and something we want may not be what is best for us.   JAB

Bless My Words, Lord (Saturday)

"The Lord was with Samuel as he grew up, and he let none of his words fall to the ground" (1 Sam. 3:19).

Hi Lord. If you couldn't tell already, I'm pretty nervous right now. Here it is already Saturday, and I have to do part of the sermon at the youth service tomorrow. I haven't even started yet. What's even worse is that I don't even understand the text. I can see it now—I'll get into the pulpit with nothing to say, and everyone will laugh at me.

I need help. I know I won't be handling this all by myself, because you will be speaking through me. I'm asking you to bless me with your words, so others may learn from them—including me.   JAB

Week 4   Matthew 3:1-17
The Late Bloomer (Sunday)

Kathy thought it was neat to have Pastor Simes teaching their Sunday school class. This week they were studying about how John the Baptist baptized Jesus. Someone got to talking about repenting and being saved, and as they went around the class, almost everyone else had had some sort of religious experience—at a church camp or at a worship service or *somewhere*. Kathy had had no such experience. She felt deprived.

Kathy wanted to talk to Pastor Simes about this. She hung back a bit after class. Pastor Simes, God bless him, always had a sharp eye for a kid who was hanging back or who was hung up inside. "Hey Kathy," he said, "help me carry these books up to my office, will you?"

When they were in the office, Kathy said, "Pastor, I—" She swallowed hard.

"I know," he said. "I could tell. What is it?"

They talked. She told her pastor that she wondered about her faith, because she had never experienced any great awakening or lightning strikes in her life.

"It's really embarrassing, being the only one—and at my age too," Kathy said.

"Jesus was a kind of late bloomer, too. His baptism was just the beginning. He was 30 and hadn't even left home yet." Kathy laughed. "Now I can't guarantee," he went on, "that the heavens will open up and there will be a dove and voices and all, like it happened with Jesus, but one day you'll know. The Spirit will be there. God may not shout. He may whisper. You'll hear it though. You'll see."

Kathy smiled. She really loved Pastor Simes. She couldn't understand why his son Steve was such a jerk.

"I guess I can wait," she said.

"Good," he said. "Let's say a prayer before you go." SS

Who Are You? (Monday)

"A voice of one calling in the desert, 'Prepare the way of the Lord' " (Matt. 3:1-2).

When the religious leaders asked John the Baptist, "Who are you?" he responded, "I am the voice of one calling in the desert, 'Make straight the way for the Lord' " (John 1:23).

John knew that his identity and purpose as a person was to draw attention to Jesus Christ. That's why he called himself a voice.

God has given you the same purpose he gave John—to draw attention to Jesus and to reflect his thoughts, attitudes, and actions in everything you say and do.　　KL

The Cross—a Reminder of Forgiveness (Tuesday)

"Confessing their sins. . . " (Matt. 3:6).

God is probably tired of forgiving me, I thought. I had been doing many wrong things, and I felt guilty and unforgivable. When I tried to tell God in prayer that I was sorry for committing these sins, I felt like a hypocrite because I knew I'd likely commit these same sins again.

Looking despondently out my bedroom window, I saw light shining in brightly distinguishable rays from the top, bottom, and sides of the moon, forming a perfect luminous cross across the night sky.

"Ask for forgiveness, repent, and you will be forgiven," I heard an inner voice say. "My child, I died on the cross for you."　　KL

What Does "Repent" Mean? (Wednesday)

"Produce fruit in keeping with repentance" (Matt. 3:8).

Repentance is admitting you have been guilty of rebelling against God and disobeying him. Hating your sin and grieving seriously on account of it is called *contrition*, the first step in repentance.

Faith—union with Christ and applying the gospel to your life—is the second step. "Give up all the evil you have been doing, and get yourselves new minds and hearts" (Ezek. 18:31 TEV).

Then "produce fruit in keeping with repentance." Change your life-style and conduct for the better. Live in Christ, and he will live in you.   KL

God's Grace Is for Everyone (Thursday)

"And do not think to say to yourselves, 'We have Abraham as our father' " (Matt. 3:9).

John the Baptist was angry that the Pharisees trusted in their descent from Abraham for salvation. The Pharisees also trusted that they would be saved because others seemed more wicked, like the cruel Romans or the people who did not worship.

God was not more willing to forgive the Pharisees simply because they were Pharisees. He forgave the Romans and the common people and the Pharisees equally. John wanted the Pharisees to realize, as we realize, that only by the love and grace of God are we saved.   KL

Adopted by God (Friday)

"This is my Son. . . " (Matt. 3:17).

"Who am I?" This is a question that all of us ask at some time. The question can be answered in many ways, but the most important answer is "a child of God."

After John baptized Jesus, God proclaimed, "This is my Son." Christians have become God's children through adoption. God adopts us into his family and loves us no less than he loves his son Jesus. Just as parents often claim children as their own by adopting them, God claimed us as his own. You are many people, but above all, as a Christian, you are God's child. That's your identity.   KL

The Empathizer (Saturday)

"Then Jesus came from Galilee to the Jordan to be baptized by John" (Matt. 3:13).

Empathize: to know how someone feels. Jesus came to earth as a man to empathize with us.

Even though Jesus had no need for the forgiveness of sin, he was baptized. Jesus asked John to baptize him so he could identify with us—poor sinners who have a need to be cleansed by the saving power of divine forgiveness.

Jesus identified with us so strongly that he gave his life for us so that we might live in eternity with him.

Jesus lived so he could identify with us. Jesus died so we might someday identify with him.   KL

Week 5   Psalm 84
Rather Be a Doorkeeper (Sunday)

Pastor Schedtler stepped in to youth group on a Sunday evening and said, "The church council would like to have at least four youth ushers for Sunday mornings."

There was a pause. Silence settled over the group like a snowfall. Sue looked around at some of the boys who would likely volunteer—Jim, who was always in church anyway, and Arnie, who would love to take old ladies by the elbow and seat them conspicuously in the third row.

The pastor spoke again. "The council asked only for youth ushers. What they didn't specify, but what *I'm* asking for, is that two of them be girls."

There was another embarrassing pause. Suddenly, strangely, Sue felt her hand go up. The pastor smiled and everyone clapped. Then several other hands popped up. Sue had been the first, the catalyst.

Her hand had gone up partly because the pauses were becoming embarrassing for Pastor Schedtler, and Sue was sensitive to embarrassment. She volunteered also partly as an escape from the beach and surfing. Several of her friends had been calling her almost every Sunday morning when the surf was up. She was becoming unchurched in great waves.

What Sue learned in the next six months was that you could be an unchurched usher too. After everyone was in and the doors were shut, she and Ann could sit in back and talk, or they could walk around to the side entrance and visit with Jim and Arnie, or they could walk down to the Fireside Room and eat a few of the cookies set out for adult forum.

There were some great things about being a doorkeeper—like meeting the people and helping them and doing it together with Ann, but worship was more then just being there every Sunday—a lot more.   SS

Lovely People (Monday)

"How lovely is your dwelling place, O Lord Almighty!" (Ps. 84:1).

I walked into the building Monday morning. There were rows of empty pews and neatly stacked hymnals. There was an altar and a pulpit. There were no people anywhere. It didn't matter that it was a church. It was Monday. Did the Lord dwell here?

I rode on a bus of happy, excited people. Everyone was smiling. Someone in the back started belting out an old-fashioned Sunday school song. Soon the whole bus joined in. The way they praised the Lord so enthusiastically made the whole bus seem lovely. It didn't matter that it was an old bus—the Lord dwelled there, in those people.   SD

Those Who Dwell (Tuesday)

"Blessed are those who dwell in your house; they are ever praising you" (Ps. 84:4).

Whenever we sing in church, I feel very self-conscious. A good voice is not one of the gifts God has given me! As I look around the church, I see other people who also look self-conscious, only for different reasons. Some are dressed differently, and some are not in church very often. Yet even though these people may feel left out or looked down on, it's not God excluding them. God's blessing includes them as much as it includes the well-dressed, perfectly-pitched soprano next to them. God hasn't blessed me with a beautiful voice, but I've been blessed in many other ways. God's blessings reach out to each of us.   SD

More (Wednesday)

"Blessed are those whose strength is in you" (Ps. 84:5).

"Did you hear? There's going to be a party. Sounds like a real good time! Are you going, Kristen?"

"No, I don't care for that kind of fun. I can find something else to do."

"You're such a *loser*! You don't know how to have fun! Come on, I'll show you a good time!"

"I've seen your 'good time' and it's not for me. There's got to be something better."

"I can't believe you! Don't you know there's more to life, Kristen!"

"There's a lot more. I'll see you around."   SD

It's OK to Pray (Thursday)

"Hear my prayer, O Lord God Almighty" (Ps. 84:8).

Whenever I hear sirens or see the flashing lights of emergency vehicles, I say a quick prayer for whoever they're racing to help. It was after one of these prayers that I looked up into two intent hazel eyes. Their elderly owner questioned me, "Were you praying?" There was a hint of disbelief in her voice. I nodded. "Aren't you a teenager?"

I wanted to scream to all the world, "Hey! It's OK to pray if you're a teenager!" I wanted to make people realize kids aren't all bad. We do pray, and God has promised to hear us. My voice won't carry to all corners of the earth, but I can start by telling you: it's OK to be a teenager who prays!   SD

Promises (Friday)

"No good thing does he withhold from those whose walk is blameless" (Ps. 84:11).

Chad had just broken up with his third girl in two months. He was sick of the feeling that crept into his stomach each time this happened. All he wanted was someone he could talk with, and most importantly, share his faith with. He couldn't understand why God didn't answer this prayer.

When Chad and Joe came to this verse in their Bible study, Chad shared his frustrations. Joe explained, "God doesn't fulfill all his promises in this life. God does have a plan for you, and if that sort of a relationship is part of it, you'll find it. Sometimes it's hard, but be open to what God wants for you, Chad—not what you want." SD

Trusting Our Lives to the Lord (Saturday)

"O Lord Almighty, blessed is the man who trusts in you" (Ps. 84:12).

Recipe for: LIFE

Ingredients: Faith, Strength, Forgiveness, Love, Thankfulness, and Trust

Note to Cook: *If you have trouble finding the ingredients, I recommend going to Prayer. They always have them on hand, and if you ask the Grocer, they're free.*

Directions: Mix Faith, Strength, Forgiveness, and Love in a large bowl. Work them together, and they will grow to be powerful. Add Thankfulness often, and you'll see how much you really have. If anything seems too much to handle, pour on the Trust. When you've added enough Trust, turn it over to the Lord. He always makes it turn out right! SD

Week 6 Jonah 1:1—4:11
Run to, Not From (Sunday)

Jonah tried to run away from a problem. He got on a boat and took off. Like almost everyone who runs away, Jonah took the trouble along with him and caused trouble for those around him.

The ultimate running away is suicide. It has become a national epidemic among teenagers. Suicide may seem a lonely and isolated solution to a bunch of lonely and isolated problems—but just talk with family and friends of a suicide victim, even years later, and watch the anguish and guilt that are still oozing out.

Maybe that's why the Bible comes down so hard on self-destruction, because it's so cruel to others and because it denies the central truth of the Bible: that God loves me and that he gave his Son for me.

How could I ever consider my life hopeless when Jesus was nailed to a cross to give me hope? How could I ever consider my life friendless when God sent Jesus to be my own personal and special friend?

So, when life begins to be depressing or hopeless, don't pull a Jonah and run away. Run, rather, into the waiting arms of Jesus. Strangely enough, you will find those arms belong not to Jesus himself, but to one of his other friends, like a classmate, your pastor, a counselor, your family doctor, your mom or dad.

Don't run away. In this life we Christians help each other. When your turn comes to need help, run *for* it, not away from it.   SS

Running Away (Monday)

"But Jonah ran away from the Lord" (Jonah 1:3).

Jeff didn't want to go back to his aunt's house and apologize for breaking an expensive vase. Instead of doing what his mom told him, he went someplace else.

His feelings were probably close to mine. I have a tendency to run away from any trouble I make. Throughout my childhood, whenever I realized I had done an awful thing, I gave myself two choices: running away or escaping through sleep. I used to take the second solution, although it didn't help at all. But in my spiritual life I can't run away from God, nor can I escape through sleep, because God is inside me. The only solution is to return to God and ask for forgiveness. THP

Distress (Tuesday)

"When my life was ebbing away, I remembered you, Lord" (Jonah 2:7).

"No presents! No Christmas! Is that clear?" Clara yelled as she slammed the newspapers on the coffee table. The recent divorce made her depressed and angry. Nearby, her three-year-old son sat on the couch, sobbing.

The tears of her child softened her heart. He made her remember a special baby who was born in this season a long time ago. "Baby Jesus, please grant me a small miracle," Clara muttered. "Please give me enough strength to endure my problems."

Holding the child in her arms, she gave him a faint smile and spoke softly, "I'm sorry. I didn't mean it, son. Perhaps God is listening to our misery right now and is trying to help us."

The boy stopped crying. He looked at his mother and laughed as she hummed, "Silent night, holy night. . . ."

THP

Thanksgiving in Time of Distress (Wednesday)

"But I, with a song of thanksgiving, will sacrifice to you. Salvation comes from the Lord" (Jonah 2:9).

Because my mother was a Christian, she used to encourage me to pray before going to bed. At first, this annoyed me. But as I came to understand the true meaning of prayer, it became a vital part of my daily activity.

In the past, most of my prayers had been asking for something. I had rarely thanked God for what he had done for me. Especially in my deepest despair, I had found it very difficult to express my thanks and to put my complete trust in God. At such times it was hard to remember all the wonderful things God had done for me. Yet my mother taught me that using a prayer of thanks in times like that puts me in a closer relationship with God. Then I too can proclaim, "Salvation comes from the Lord."   THP

Let God Be the Judge (Thursday)

"[God] had compassion and did not bring upon them the destruction he had threatened" (Jonah 3:10).

After my watch was stolen in the locker room, I couldn't trust anybody. Everyone around me looked suspicious.

"Why doesn't God destroy all the evil people?" I complained to my dad one day. "How can God let them live and do bad things like stealing my watch?"

"Because God is merciful, son," my father spoke gently. "Everyone is sinful, including you and me, so we shouldn't pass judgment on others. Would you like to be put down for every little thing you did?" he asked.

"Of course not, dad."

"Then when someone does wrong, son, let God be the final judge."   THP

Misuse of God's Gifts (Friday)

"Let them give up their evil ways and their violence" (Jonah 3:8).

On August 8, 1945, the first atomic bomb was dropped on Hiroshima, Japan. The world had entered the nuclear age. Now we are all faced with the question, How will we use the power locked in the atom? Can we use it safely to generate electricity? Can it be used to benefit people through medical research? Or will it be used for nuclear war?

God has given to humankind earth's energy, power, and many more good resources. God also expects his people to use them to fulfill their physical needs as well as to aid others. However, we misuse these resources and turn them into evil destructive means.

We need to ask for God's forgiveness for the misuse of his gifts. We can also ask God to help us turn from our evil ways, to love and trust one another.   THP

God Is the Greatest Parent (Saturday)

"You are a gracious and compassionate God, slow to anger, and abounding in love" (Jonah 4:2).

Tim loved his parents. They were the most fantastic parents he had ever known. They were kind, gentle, understanding, and they were slow to become angry.

Many times Tim's disobedience hurt his parents. He didn't go to school. He didn't mow the lawn. He had a fight with his friend, and he let the dog go hungry while his parents were gone. But they still loved their son. Through their example, Tim came to know another Parent, one much greater than all the parents in this world—God. God cares and loves not only Tim's family, but the whole human race.   THP

Week 7   Luke 4:14-30
Hometown Boy (Sunday)

When Dan came back home from college, his friends could see he was different. He walked differently, he wore his clothes and his hair differently, he talked differently; but most of all, he acted differently.

"Who does he think he is?" Bucky asked. "Where does he come off trying to tell us what to do?"

"He wasn't trying to tell us what to do," Beth said. "He just said he didn't want to do it. He didn't, either."

"That's just it," Bucky broke in. "He used to be right along on all our stuff. Does he think he's too fancy for us, just because he's been off to college?"

"Marty's been to college too," Andy added. "But he's the same as ever. How can two guys come back to town so different after just a year of college?"

"They were different before," Beth said.

"They were not," Bucky objected.

"They were too. Dan never really enjoyed some of the dumb stuff we do. He went along, but he never liked it. College just gave him the strength to say no."

"Next thing you know he'll be preaching to us, telling us what to do."

"Might be good for us sometimes," Beth said. "Everybody ought to get out of this stupid town for a while. Maybe we'd all be better off."

"Just let him try changing me," Bucky said, spitting in the grass.

"You should have been born in Nazareth. You'd have pushed him over the cliff."

"Pushed who?"

"Jesus."

"See! What'd I tell you. He's got Beth talking religion."   SS

Search for Sight (Monday)

"He has sent me to proclaim . . . recovering of sight for the blind" (Luke 4:18).

Jerry peered hazily over the top of the *Tribune. Same old news,* he thought, and threw the sports section down. He slumped over the kitchen table and pushed his hands to his temple, trying to make the thoughts come out. *What is wrong?* he wondered. *What do I need?*

What Jerry needs is a new attitude toward life—the kind of new attitude that Christ can give. Sometimes it's not the world around us that gives us trouble, but the world inside us. The heart is often the place where sight can be found.   DW

A Constant Fulfillment (Tuesday)

"Today this scripture is fulfilled in your hearing" (Luke 4:21).

"Today" is always changing, and is always in the present. The miracles of Jesus are always in the present too. The Scripture is constantly being fulfilled.

The miracles of old were spectacular—a man walked on water, a few bits of bread fed hundreds. The miracles of today are no less wonderful. A woman is instantly cured of cancer, or a beggar finds a mound of cash. On a smaller scale, the very fact that we wake up each morning breathing the air of God's world is something of a miracle. We experience miracles, large and small, every day, and all are worthy of thanks. Thank God for miracles!   DW

Doubting Is Easy (Wednesday)

"Physician, heal yourself!" (Luke 4:23).

The magician waved his magic wand over the table and pulled away the handkerchief. The pigeon disappeared. *"Now* do you believe?" he demanded.

"One more time," Jill replied.

The magician sighed, and began again. Jill leaned closer, secretly hoping he'd make a mistake. She believed in his powers while he was performing, but when he finished the trick, she forgot she had believed.

Do we have to doubt the power of God? Many times we can't see how the power is working in this world. That's OK. Just so we believe that it *is* working. Proof is for doubters; faith is for believers.   DW

Truth Challenge (Thursday)

"No prophet is accepted in his home town" (Luke 4:24).

Ted sold Bibles door to door. The one thing that kept him enthusiastic about the job year after year was truth— the truth of the Word of God.

When Ted came to a town, he wouldn't just *sell* the truth, he would *tell* the truth. He wasn't greeted warmly everywhere he went, because some of what he told sank deep and rang terribly, honestly true.

Sometimes we deny the truth even when it is staring us in the face. We retaliate against the prophets of truth when we hear what we'd rather not. Standing up for the truth is a challenge we ought to try to accept, with the help of God.   DW

Godshare (Friday)

"And there were many in Israel with leprosy. . . yet none of them was cleansed—only Naaman the Syrian" (Luke 4:27).

Loving God is a good deal. You can be on a one-to-one basis and trade information (mostly questions from you, answers from God). This personal business is a nice part of the relationship.

There's a chance for problems to crop up, however. If you get caught up in this "fun" side of being close to God, you may feel as if you have sole claim on him. Jesus rebuked the Israelites for feeling this way. God does not belong to anyone, but is available to everyone. We can love—but cannot own—God.   DW

On the Side of the Power (Saturday)

"But he walked right through the crowd and went on his way" (Luke 4:30).

I would run, and my dog would come with me. On one of our jaunts we came across a pair of neighbor dogs. The two looked ready to run the stranger straight off the property, so I started to drag my dog away. Then he surprised me. Instead of bristling into a defense, he gave them a countering, humbling stare. They slinked off, and we ran on.

Why wasn't Jesus hurt as he walked through the angry crowd? I think they didn't dare touch him. Like my dog, Jesus gave them an indication of his power, and they bowed quietly to it. Be glad that Jesus loves sinners like us! It is terrifying for the proud to feel his mighty stare!

DW

Week 8   John 2:1-11
Do Whatever He Tells You (Sunday)

There are people we instinctively trust.

A football coach says to a guard practicing a trap play, "Pivot on your outside foot. Explode in just behind your tackle low and fast." The player tries it in Friday's game and makes several bone-jarring key blocks.

A band director says, "Come in on the back side of the beat and sharp it slightly." The solo is superb.

The driver's ed instructor says, "Steer toward the skid." You hit an oil slick, remember her advice, and you don't go in the ditch.

Not all advice is good. Nor is all advice serious—even from Jesus: "If your eye offend you, pluck it out." Our job as Christians, young and old, is to find those who can give us good advice—then take it, trying our best to do whatever he or she tells us. If it works, we pass it on.

By the time they went to the Cana wedding, Mary already knew that Jesus could work miracles. She told the servants to obey him. "Do whatever he tells you," she said. Some of us have had miracles worked in our lives. Maybe Jesus has transformed us in some way—fixed our loneliness or despair, healed our broken hearts, built bridges between us and our parents or family, healed our ills. If we have known his miracles, we ought to share that, pass it on. We ought to say to those who haven't tried his way, "Do whatever he tells you." That's good advice, you know.   SS

Jesus the Man (Monday)

"Jesus and his disciples had also been invited to the wedding" (John 2:2).

The next time you're at a party, wedding, or a gathering with your friends, remember that Jesus did the same thing once.

Maybe you're thinking that he was too busy with his miracles and stuff to go to weddings. But he did go.

Even though we know today how special Jesus is, when he was alive, he was an ordinary person, like you and me.   TLM

Patience—Respected Virtue (Tuesday)

"Jesus replied, 'My time has not yet come' " (John 2:4).

When urging Mary to be patient, Jesus gave us a hint of what was to come.

Sometimes today we want instant answers. When those instant answers are not available, we become upset and impatient.

Just as Jesus urged Mary to be patient, we should also be patient.

So the next time you're looking for that instant answer, remember that all things will come in due time.
                                                          TLM

Mary's Advice (Wednesday)

"Do whatever he tells you" (John 2:5).

You have a major decision to make, and you don't know what to do. You've tried to work it out on your own, but you couldn't do it.

Try talking to God! Whenever we need help, God is there for us. Perhaps Mary was giving us some advice when she told the servants to do whatever Jesus told them. Though we rarely hear of God talking directly to people today, God often talks to us through our friends, parents, and pastors. Through these people God is helping us to work out our problems.

Why turn down good advice? TLM

From Words to Faith (Thursday)

"Fill the jars with water" (John 2:7).

Jesus told the servants to fill the jars with water. Then he changed that water into wine, making it better than before.

Today Jesus still tells his servants to fill containers. He tells teachers to fill their students, pastors to fill their congregations, and us to fill our friends. He wants all of us to fill people with the message of God's love.

In a way Jesus is filling us with God's Word. Then he changes that Word into faith, and our faith into words that will help others to know him as we do. TLM

A Touch of Gold (Friday)

"The master of the banquet tasted the water that had been turned into wine" (John 2:9).

King Midas, legend tells us, had a touch of gold which he used for greed. Two thousand years ago there was a man who had a similar ability. Everything he touched turned richer and better. He could heal the sick and renew those who had lost their faith.

Even today, when he comes into our lives, we are made richer, just as the water became richer in the form of wine.

Who is this man?

Jesus, the man with a touch of gold.   TLM

What If They Realized? (Saturday)

"The servants who had drawn the water knew" (John 2:9).

When Jesus turned water into wine, only the servants knew he had done it. Those servants knew Jesus changed the water, but they may not have known who Jesus was or what he was destined to do.

Today we know who Jesus is and what he can and has done for us. Jesus has entered our plain lives, and like the water, they have been changed, transformed.

Imagine the difference if the servants had known who Jesus was. Imagine the difference that can be since we *do* know who Jesus is!   TLM

Week 9 Matthew 4:1-11
Risking Your Life (Sunday)

"Make bread; risk your life; get rich quick." Pauline said the words right out loud as she laid the Bible down. She was reading about Jesus' temptation in the wilderness. Satan had come to him and tempted him three ways: make bread, risk your life, and get rich quick.

Pauline closed her eyes and saw her father out on the 18-wheeler. She had ridden with him sometimes last summer, but lately he seemed to be driven to drive, to be driven by the devil. He broke ICC rules about hours on the road; he took jobs to strange locations and at strange times. Could money be that important, could bread? Could his life be worth so little?

It was different before, when her mother was alive. Sure, they both worked. Sure, her income took some of the load off her dad, but no one in the family wanted him to kill himself just so they could have *things*. They had bread enough and plenty. He could stay home some weekends. He could refuse some of the risky jobs.

It was Sunday morning, time for church. Her dad hadn't been to church in months, she knew it. He was always on the road. He would call in at noon, though. He always did. She would pray for him. She would pray now and at church, and later, too, just before he called. She would pray that Satan might get his icky claws out of her father, that her father wouldn't risk his life just to get bread and to get rich quick.

When he called later, she would tell him that she loved him, and that she had been praying for him, and that she didn't want him to risk his life anymore.   SS

And Lead Us Not into Temptation (Monday)

"Then Jesus was led by the Spirit. . . to be tempted by the devil" (Matt. 4:1).

Do we recognize the importance of praying "lead us not into temptation"? Daily we face temptation. "Come on, have a smoke with us!" "The teacher isn't looking; let me copy your answers!"

When we are tempted to do wrong, or to be part of wrongdoing, we need to remind ourselves of this petition and pray that God would give us courage and strength to say "No!"

Our Lord hears every prayer, and he will help us. It is so easy to forget that God is here whenever we need him, especially in times of temptation. What a privilege prayer is! Jesus, who withstood temptation, will also help us in ours.   PJR

Jesus: Truly God and Truly Human (Tuesday)

"After fasting forty days and forty nights, he was hungry" (Matt. 4:2).

How many times a day do we eat? Three meals and then some! Without food we would starve. It is part of our humanity.

This text shows us our Savior's humanity as well. He too needed to eat. In the Bible, "forty days and forty nights" is a way of saying "a long time." After a long period of fasting, Jesus must have experienced painful hunger pangs. But he fasted in order to prepare himself fully for the ordeal ahead of him—the temptations.

We know from his wondrous birth that he is truly God. And we know from his hunger that he was every bit as human as we are. That's a great comfort to us! PJR

Stones into Bread (Wednesday)

"The tempter came to him and said, 'If you are the Son of God, tell these stones to become bread' " (Matt. 4:3).

Hardly a day goes by when we do not eat bread. Bread is an important source of nutrients in our diet. We need it to stay healthy.

In the first temptation, the devil wanted Jesus to turn stones into bread. He knew that Jesus was hungry. But Jesus refused. As important as physical needs are, Jesus knew that the greater need was to do his Father's will. So he answered, "Man does not live on bread alone."

Jesus knows all our needs, both physical and spiritual. Just as he gives bread for our bodies, so he gives us his Word for our spiritual hunger. After all, isn't he "the bread of life"? That bread satisfies!   PJR

Not on Bread Alone (Thursday)

"Man does not live on bread alone" (Matt. 4:4).

God sent his Son Jesus for a specific purpose: to redeem us from sin and death by dying and rising again for us. The devil knew this also! He knew that he would lose if Jesus did his Father's will. That is why he tempted Jesus to be popular and spectacular. Anything to keep him from doing the Father's will!

But Jesus' love for us was so strong that he refused to be sidetracked. Three times he refuted Satan's temptations. Three times he proved that he knew why he had come to our earth. He came to lay down his life for all of us. He knew that there could be no victory without the cross.   PJR

An Opportune Time (Friday)

"Then the devil left him" (Matt. 4:11).

Luke's gospel adds "until an opportune time" to this verse. After tempting Jesus in the wilderness, Satan realized that Jesus was too strong. He retreated and waited "until an opportune time." He waited for Jesus to become vulnerable.

Doesn't he do the same for us? He tempts us at our weakest moments. Perhaps we have just lost a good friend, or we have had an argument with our parents. He waits for times when our faith is weakest, times when we feel as though no one cares for us or loves us.

Those are the very times we need to pray to God just as Jesus did. He will help us at "the opportune time." God will keep our faith strong.   PJR

Strength in Temptations (Saturday)

"Then the devil left him" (Matt. 4:11).

Three times Satan tempted Jesus, and three times he failed. Jesus' resolve was too strong. The devil left him, but he would return.

In our own lives Satan tempts us as well. Whenever we lie or cheat or steal or injure someone else, or whenever we fail to serve others when we have opportunity, we succumb to temptation. At such times we need to come to our Lord for his strength. He will help us. We know he has the power, because his death and resurrection won the victory over sin and death and Satan. Satan will continue tempting us, but in Christ we can conquer.   PJR

Week 10   Psalm 51
Against You, You Only (Sunday)

Elaine knew the story of David and Bathsheba, and as she practiced reading Psalm 51 for next Sunday's service, she thought about the connection between the two. *Some nerve, that David had,* she thought, *praying a psalm like that after what he did.* She recounted in her mind all the people David had sinned against and all the different kinds of sins he had committed. How could he say he had sinned against God and only God?

To begin with there was the adultery itself—his sin and her sin—then he lied, then he killed her husband, she thought. *A man was dead, the man's wife was pregnant, David's family was disrupted, and so, finally, was the whole kingdom.*

All sin might be against God, Elaine thought, *but it's not only God who gets hurt.* She thought of some recent events around town: Art's careless driving had left Diane in the hospital, while Art walked away with only a black eye. And Mr. Edwards, who had managed the Farmer's Elevator so badly that everyone in the cooperative lost money. And that contractor who went bankrupt owing her father $8,000. *We don't only sin against God,* she thought, *we sin against lots of people—and we ought to do something about that.*

Elaine then thought about the mean thing she had said about Marnie last week and how it had gotten back to Marnie and how bad she must have felt. *I'll make it up to her,* she thought. *God may have already forgiven me, but getting Marnie to forgive me will be some work.*   SS

Who's Gonna Know? (Monday)

"Against you, you only, have I sinned and done what is evil in your sight" (Ps. 51:4).

Fifty cases of M & M's and candy bars for our French Club fund raiser were delivered outside the cafeteria during the lunch period. When the candy was moved to the French room first period the next day, two cases were found missing. I can imagine the thief saying to this golden opportunity, "Who's gonna see? Who's gonna know?"

The thief sinned against the French Club by leaving them $20 short. But more important, the thief also sinned against God. When we are tempted to sin, we should remember that the one who is always "gonna see, gonna know" is God.

The wonderful part is knowing once we "come clean" and ask forgiveness, we'll be forgiven.   EMB

I'm Sorry. . . Again (Tuesday)

"Surely you desire truth in the inner parts" (Ps. 51:6).

How can God tell when we are really sorry? If I say I'll never do a certain sin again, then slip and do it, does that mean that God won't forgive me?

God wants me to be honest with myself, and with him. We both know I will sin again, and I will ask forgiveness.

It's like a little girl who goes out to play in her new dress. God can cleanse me again, just like the little girl's mother can wash her dress. Both do so out of love for the child. The fact that the little girl again wears her dress to play in may anger her mother, but she'll wash it and send the girl off with a kiss the next day.

Our sinning may anger God, but realizing we are only children (no matter how old), God will wash us clean and send us off with a kiss!   EMB

Thoughts before Sleep (Wednesday)

"Let me hear joy and gladness; let the bones you have crushed rejoice" (Ps. 51:8).

Lord, I can't seem to sleep tonight. I really try to do things you want me to, but it's hard sometimes. There's a kid at school that everyone picks on. He's "weird." Actually, he's a pretty nice guy, and he's really smart. He just wears funny clothes, or sometimes says something dumb. I want to be nice to him, but something inside me says "No!" I don't think I'd like him, because he's so weird, but I've never given him a chance.

Please help me *want* to be nice to him and remind me when I need it, that you were, in a way, the "weird kid" too, and you turned out OK! I know you love him, so please help me love him too. Next time I see him, I'll say "Hi" and give him a smile. Thanks, Lord.   EMB

Asking for Pardon (Thursday)

"Hide your face from my sins and blot out all my iniquities" (Psalm 51:9).

"Sorry isn't enough, you've ruined my new dress!" Linda's sister hollered.

For God, "sorry" *is* enough. And that's good, because even if we try, there is nothing any of us can do to deserve the complete forgiveness we are given. It is given merely because God loves us.

I used to wish I could "be good" all the time. That way I wouldn't need to be forgiven, because I'd be doing what God wanted me to. But of course, none of us can live perfect lives. We *are* in need of forgiveness. We all need the grace of God which Jesus died to win for us. Because of his death, we can say, "I'm sorry," and know that God, who loves us all, has forgiven us.   EMB

About My Brother, Lord (Friday)

"Create in me a pure heart, O God, and renew a steadfast spirit within me" (Ps. 51:10).

Lord, I don't always get along with my brother. In fact, I sometimes wish we offered human sacrifices; then I could get rid of him graciously. He's not a bad guy, though. He just rubs me the wrong way now and then. He can really get on my nerves when I'm studying, because I'm the kind of person who needs total quiet. It also bugs me when he teases me. Why can't he leave me alone?

I always feel bad when we have an argument, because I can get pretty mean sometimes. I'm sorry. You love my brother too, and I know you don't like us to fight. Please give me the patience to ignore his agitating, and the humility to apologize when I'm wrong. Thanks, Lord.

EMB

Bringing the Broken Spirit Home (Saturday)

". . . And sinners will turn back to you" (Ps. 51:13).

I know that the Lord forgives me all my sins. I also know that I don't deserve such forgiveness. Saying "I'm sorry" a hundred times wouldn't fix some of the mistakes I've made, but God knows when I'm really sorry and will forgive me anything.

That makes me wish I could do something to repay God. Maybe the best thing I can do is tell everyone that God will forgive them anything. If they're really sorry, God will know, and they'll be forgiven. It says in the psalm, "The sacrifices of God are a broken spirit." I can bring my broken spirit to God when I've done wrong, and he will mend it. I can also bring another broken spirit when I tell someone else about the forgiveness of God.

EMB

Week 11   Luke 15:11-32
Party Noises (Sunday)

"My brother was out in the field when I came home. He was still there when the party started. The neighbors had begun to come over; the family was gathered; the calf was roasting. Then he came home—and now he won't even come in.

"Talk about a party pooper. Sure, I was wrong. Sure, I ran away and blew a pot of dough—and that's not all either. But I came back. I'm here. I wish I could tell him how lonely I was out there, and how I was willing to come back as a hired man. I'd have done anything he told me to do. I'd have been his slave. I really would.

"But dad wouldn't have it. Dad wanted me back to work *with* them, not *for* them—father and son, brother and brother, side by side. I suppose that's part of what's eating my brother. I never liked the work much before. I wasn't much help. He did most of it. But that's going to change.

"Being taken back does change a person. I was all set for hard work and the bunkhouse—and an angry father. What I got was my old room back and love—at least from father. I guess brother can't handle that part either. I'm the one who fouled it all up, and now I'm getting all the love—clothes, jewelry, a party—the whole works. No wonder he's ticked.

"But I *will* show him. I will even if he stays out there and grumps, even if he cold-shoulders me at first. I'll win him over. I'll work hard. I'll do it his way. I'll take his advice. I'll love him. That will do it. He can't resist that. He can't."   SS

To Breathe or Not to Breathe (Monday)

"The younger son got together all he had, set off for a distant country and there squandered his wealth in wild living" (Luke 15:13).

God is like air. No matter what I do, I can't live without him for long. Oh, I've tried! But it's like stopping breathing: not too good—terminal, in fact.

God made us to be with him. It's our purpose. But it's easy to forget that sometimes. We think we can manage on our own. We forget all about God. But then we get a little dizzy, the world starts to spin, and we find ourselves on the floor. The wonderful thing is that no matter how many times I turn away from God, whenever I turn back he doesn't leave me to suffocate but fills my lungs up with air again! PAF

Ceaseless Giving (Tuesday)

"So he divided his property between them. . . 'Quick! Bring the best robe, and put it on him' " (Luke 15:12, 22).

Understand:
I love you.
Is that not reason enough?
What more do you want?
There is no more to want,
to even imagine.
Return to me.
Then be still
and accept.
I will give and give and give to you.
I am not foolish:
I am who I am.   PAF

Dancing Lessons (Wednesday)

"Let's have a feast and celebrate. For this son of mine was dead and is alive again" (Luke 15:23-24).

Look!
God dances!
Such powerful joy
in each holy step.
Why does God dance today?
See who returns from the fog?
One of his children whom Satan took.
God sings him the triumphant song:
"I love you! Come stay.
No grudge is kept."
Kissing his boy,
God prances!
Look!

PAF

The Most Important Thing (Thursday)

"The older brother became angry and refused to go in" (Luke 15:28).

"Kathy," Anna said, "you're my best friend and I need to tell you something. I've been involved. . . in homosexuality. But I've repented, and I want to change." The words *repented* and *change* mattered most, but Kathy froze at "homosexuality."

"I believe now that I shouldn't have done it, that it was wrong," Anna said, "but Christ died for this sin, too. I can change—even if the change isn't complete until I'm with him in heaven! It won't be easy, though. I'll need your support."

"Get out of my sight!" was all Kathy could say.

Alone later, Anna thought about the rebuff. "Oh, it hurts! Kathy may never forgive me! But I must remember that God has forgiven me, and *that's* what's most important."

PAF

Prodigal Sons and Daughters, Inc. (Friday)

"You are always with me, and everything I have is yours" (Luke 15:31).

Dear Prospective Prodigal:

Are your parents tyrants? Are your brothers and sisters impossible? Are your teachers tedious? Are you dying to be *out on your own?*

No matter what your discontent, we at Prodigal Sons and Daughters, Inc. have the staff to help you. Prodigals themselves, each staff member knows just how you feel and has plenty of experience to help you meet your needs. Our only rule is, "If it feels good, do it."

Rubbish! I know that even though life isn't always fun, God *is* with me, and having made me, knows *exactly* what I need and will meet those needs. I don't need anyone else but God.   PAF

The Gift (Saturday)

"I will set out and go back to my father" (Luke 15:18).

She wouldn't look at me.

"Who are you to be so proud that you think the blood of God's own perfect Son isn't enough for you?" I asked. "Or that God isn't big enough to forgive you?"

"I don't deserve forgiveness!" she said.

"Exactly! It's a gift. Gifts aren't deserved, they're just given. It's called grace." She continued to stare at the floor.

"God wants to give you peace. This despair is garbage! God loves you!"

"Why?"

"Because God wants to. All that is asked is for you to love him back."

She smiled.   PAF

Week 12   Genesis 28:10-22

Sleeping on a Rock (Sunday)

"Mom, you gotta hear this."

"Hear what?"

"Karleen's home from Sunday school with a story about Jacob sleeping on a rock."

"It's in the Bible. What's wrong with that?"

"She's out in the garden right now looking for a rock to use for a pillow."

"How very interesting."

"According to Karleen's Sunday school book Jacob slept on a rock and had the vision of the ladder—and then the Lord spoke to him."

"What's it all got to do with you?"

"I'm going to laugh my head off. She's going to sleep on a rock and see if the Lord will speak to *her*."

"He might, you know."

"Aw, mom!"

"You know what Jesus said about becoming like a child."

"Not like Karleen. Not me."

"She's only six. Her faith is pretty specialized."

"But sleeping on a rock? Come on, mom."

"You *won't* laugh—and neither will any of us. Someday, years from now, we may all laugh about this, but we won't laugh now. *Do you hear?*"

"I hear. OK."

"What did Jacob do with the rock afterwards?"

"In her book it says they made an altar out of it."

"Then that's what we'll do. Tomorrow morning, whether she has had her dreams or not, we'll set that rock on top of Granny's German Bible. It will be the most special rock in this country. Here she comes. Now don't laugh."

"I'll try not to."   SS

Blessing (Monday)

"All peoples on earth will be blessed through you and your offering" (Gen. 28:14).

BE A BLESSING!

You've heard others talk about their experiences! You've wondered if it was for you! *Now,* through this special offer, *you* can learn the formula! No gimmicks! Nothing to buy!

Simply follow these instructions:

1. Look to God for guidance.
2. Look within for desire.
3. Look around for need.
4. Look for ways to put it together.

No risk to you! You may cancel at any time!

SATISFACTION GUARANTEED   KK

Care (Tuesday)

"I am with you and will watch over you wherever you go" (Gen. 28:15)

Morning radio news is bad.
My mom's a grouch and so's my dad.
I flunked a test. My best friend's mad.
Lord, will you take care of me?

The acne's back. My room's a sight.
I can't get a date for Saturday night.
All my clothes are a size too tight.
Lord, will you take care of me?

It's when little things seem so hard,
When I've lost my keys and my library card,
When my hair needs a cut and so does the yard,
I know the Lord takes care of me.   KK

A Long Time (Wednesday)

"I will not leave you. . ." (Gen. 28:15).

Some things are hard to avoid:
- that icky you-know-who with a crush on you,
- your great-aunt's wet kisses,
- your mom the morning after you got home late.

Some things are hard to get rid of:
- pimples,
- little sisters who tag along,
- everybody's stories about you at that party.

Some things seem to last forever:
- English class,
- waiting in the lunch line,
- the eternities when you are grounded.

Jesus will be with you longer than *that*.   KK

Mine (Thursday)

"Of all that you give me I will give you a tenth" (Gen. 28:22).

A man named John spent his life in dark shafts digging coal. One day, the tunnel caved in and blocked the air supply. Everyone shook their heads and said, "It was the mine that did him in."

Another man named John was a soldier. One day he took a walk across a field and was never seen again. Everyone shook their heads and said, "It was a mine that did him in."

A third man named John was very healthy. He saved his money, invested it wisely, and *never* shared it with anyone. Everyone shook their heads. It was the "mine" that did him in.   KK

Losing It (Friday)

"Surely the Lord is in this place, and I was not aware of it" (Gen. 28:16).

You can lose a lot of things.
   Some of them aren't very important:
   ● the gross sweater your mother made you wear,
   ● the appointment card that tells you when to go back to the orthodontist.
   Others are kind of important:
   ● the last two tickets to Saturday's football game
   ● your father's keys when he's late for work.
   A few things are really important:
   ● your self-respect,
   ● the feeling that somebody cares.
You can never lose God. God always cares.   KK

Sanctuary (Saturday)

"This is none other than the house of God" (Gen. 28:17).

Silent prayers, lifted hearts

Are at peace there.

Not a building, not a room,

Church is people. One mind

Together, giving strength

Until each soul

Alone can face the day,

Remembering that

Yahweh is at home anywhere.   KK

Week 13   John 11:1-53
Letting Your Friend Die (Sunday)

Lazarus was probably Jesus' best friend. Among the disciples it was Peter, or maybe John, but among ordinary people certainly Lazarus was the most special—as were his sisters, Mary and Martha.

That's what must have made Jesus' decision seem so strange to his disciples. Word came to Jesus that Lazarus was deathly ill. Now you'd think that if they were best friends, Jesus would have packed up and hustled off to Bethany to heal him. He didn't. Strange.

Jesus stayed two days longer before he started out. How about that? Even today, when we are all so busy, that would be unheard of. "Your best friend's critically ill in the hospital." "Oh, I'll pop around in a few days." "Your brother's been in a serious accident." "Well, I'll call in a few days and find out how he is."

Jesus, of course, hung back so Lazarus *would* die. The miracle was preplanned. You and I don't have that option. If grandma dies before we get around to visiting her, we can't bring her back for another try. If a friend is sick or injured, we need to be there right away so she knows how much we care—and so we can be of help.

Postponing right decisions and acts of kindness is not safe. People die out from under us; people move away; they give up waiting; they misunderstand. When we procrastinate, we sometimes miss forever those prime chances to help and care and share. There is a "do it now" urgency about many things. Don't delay!   SS

Panic (Monday)

"Yet when he heard that Lazarus was sick, he stayed where he was two more days" (John 11:6).

Once when I was alone in my house, I started to choke on some food. I quickly tried some first aid steps and got the food out of my throat. Lucky that I didn't panic—that could have been dangerous!

When Jesus heard about Lazarus being ill, he didn't panic or get all excited. He even waited two days. Martha couldn't understand why Jesus did this.

Perhaps if we could see things through the eyes of Jesus we would have a different perspective. Jesus deals with matters in his own relaxed and confident way. We may not understand God's timing, but we can trust him to act at the right time. AW

In God We Trust (Tuesday)

" 'But Rabbi,' they said, 'a short while ago the Jews tried to stone you, and yet you are going back there?' " (John 11:8).

When Jesus went back to see Lazarus in Bethany, he could have been stoned to death by the hostile people of that town. Yet he still went to see Lazarus. He carried no weapons to protect him, but he had a more powerful protection than any weapon. He trusted in God.

Our faith and trust in God gives us courage. We are never alone. God is always there, ready to help us.

We can put our trust in him. AW

The Blind Can See (Wednesday)

"A man who walks by day will not stumble, for he sees by this world's light" (John 11:9).

A blind pastor preached a sermon about how we are under God's protection. He quoted, "A man who walks by day will not stumble, for he sees by this world's light."

After church he was asked, "Is it hard for you to talk about the light of the world when you are blind?"

The pastor said, "No. Even though I cannot see the light of the world, I can feel it. God shines his light of guidance and protection on everyone. If we accept God's help, he will not let us go astray, but lead us in the right direction."   AW

Being There (Thursday)

"Then Thomas (called Didymus) said to the rest of the disciples, 'Let us also go, that we may die with him' " (John 11:16).

Thomas wanted to go with Jesus to Lazarus's tomb. He was willing to face death at the hands of the hostile people of Bethany in order to be with Jesus. Is that what friendship is?

When I know friends are hurting or facing some special trial, I want to stand by them.

Being a Christian friend means more than praying for the friend; it means getting involved. It means action. It means being there.

"Let us also go. . . ."   AW

Have Hope (Friday)

"But I know that even now God will give you whatever you ask" (John 11:22).

It's hard to move to another town. I have moved three times. Each time was disappointing, because I was leaving friends and home behind. But I still hoped that I would meet new friends and live in a nice town. It always turned out that way.

I think disappointment ties in with hope. When Martha saw Jesus after Lazarus died, she was disappointed in him because he was late, but she still had hope in him that he could save Lazarus.

When disappointment comes, rather than blaming God or others, it is best to look for the signs of hope, trusting that God will help us.   AW

Life after Death (Saturday)

"Martha answered, 'I know he will rise again in the resurrection at the last day' " (John 11:24).

A friend of mine died of leukemia. The end came after five months of battling the disease. It was devastating for her family and all of us who loved her so much. After her death I asked God, "Why couldn't you save her from death as you saved Lazarus? Why?"

Instead of an answer, I received comfort in knowing that even though God doesn't heal every dying Christian, he gives them the gift of eternal life. Few people like Lazarus are brought back to life on earth, but all who are Christians will have eternal life.   AW

Week 14   John 4:1-42
Drawing Water at Noon (Sunday)

There might have been a dozen reasons why this Samaritan woman came at noon: an illness, an unexpected childbirth in the neighborhood, unexpected guests. Why did she brave the noonday heat to do her hardest work of the day? At dusk there would have been crowds of women at the well. By then most of them would have finished their day, and come there to attend the town forum. Jacob's well was a place of gossip, chatting, and friendly exchange.

Or maybe the woman came at noon to avoid all that. Maybe she wanted to be alone. Maybe she didn't feel like sharing herself and her secrets with the town biddies. Maybe she was different, more free, more thoughtful than the others. Or maybe it was guilt.

Everyone sometimes needs to be alone. We all have times when we want to climb the water tower at midnight and just sit there and think about the town, its people, or about ourselves. There are times when we like to slip into the front pew on a Monday afternoon and enjoy the silence of God, alone. There are times we want to stroll in the park or along the riverbank by ourselves. Jesus did it often.

But too much loneliness isn't good. We are created as people of the pack. We are made to be with each other. Being alone needs to be balanced off with being together. If you are too much alone, talk to your pastor about it, or your school counselor, or an adult friend. We can learn to keep our times under control. We can learn to be together. We can even learn to draw our water in the chatty atmosphere of the evening crowds.   SS

The Man Who Ignores Reputations (Monday)

Jesus said to her, "Will you give me a drink?" (John 4:7).

Picture yourself in Samaria about 2000 years ago. It is around noon on the hottest day of the summer. Everyone has taken shade from the scorching sun and agonizing dust—except for one woman standing in the blistering heat, drawing water from Jacob's well. She is a woman with a bad reputation and not accepted by the public. There is also a man standing next to her asking for a drink. Despite her reputation, he still treats her as he would any other person.

This man accepted everyone—whether they had good or bad reputations—during his life on earth, and he still does to this day.   JAB

A Real Friend (Tuesday)

"You are a Jew and I am a Samaritan woman. How can you ask me for a drink?" (John 4:9)

I was not very well accepted when I was in junior high. I didn't smoke, didn't hang around the "right" people, and I was a Christian. My own self-confidence became so low that I often thought of myself as worthless. Then in ninth grade a very pretty, well-liked girl came up and talked to me as if I were one of her friends. She didn't care who I was or what I looked like; she accepted me the way I was. She also helped me become more self-confident.

Christ accepts each of us the same way the girl accepted me—no matter how we feel about ourselves.

JAB

Thirst (Wednesday)

"Whoever drinks of the water I give him will never thirst" (John 4:14).

With sweat beading on my forehead and my mouth as dry as a sunscorched desert, I continue the three-mile race. My eyes are focused on what is three strides ahead of me, and my mind is dreaming of the water at the end of the race. Right now I would love to take a drink of some "supernatural" water that would keep me as strong at the end of the race as I was at the beginning, but no water like that exists.

There is, though, a form of refreshment that will keep us strong spiritually. The water Christ provides to us will quench our spiritual thirst forever.   JAB

Fountain of Eternal Life (Thursday)

"The water I give him will become in him a spring of water welling up to eternal life" (John 4:14).

Ponce de Leon was probably the most noted of the many explorers who searched for the "Fountain of Youth." He traveled the world for many years in search of this coveted spring.

There is another fountain that people search for just as eagerly. It is the "Fountain of Eternal Life." Yet God offered us this fountain when he sent his only Son to earth to die for our sins.

You don't need to be like Ponce de Leon and search the world for this spring, for if you accept God's Word as truth, you can find this fountain in your own heart. JAB

The Human Harvest (Friday)

"Even now the reaper draws his wages, even now he harvests the crop for eternal life" (John 4:36).

One September while flying over eastern Washington just before harvest time I saw a landscape covered with velvety wheat fields. What an incredible job it must be to prepare and plant all those square miles of fields! It must take every farmhand to do the work.

People who have not accepted God's Word are like empty fields. There are so many, and they all need someone to sow their field. It takes every farmhand to do the work of telling God's Word so more people may receive the gift of everlasting life.　　　　JAB

You Gotta See It to Believe It (Saturday)

"We no longer believe just because of what you said; now we have heard for ourselves" (John 4:42).

I guess I've always taken Mount Rainier for granted. It was always just a mountain to me. One day my brother invited me to go climbing on it. "You've got to see it to believe it," he coaxed.

I soon found myself at the beginning of the mountain trail. Before long I was convinced that I did have to see it to believe it. Never in my life had I seen anything as majestic.

Oftentimes God's love is similar to Mount Rainier for me. I see it every day, yet I take it for granted. God's love is too great to be taken for granted. God loves and cares for us so much that he sent his only Son to die for every one of us.　　　　JAB

Blue Funk (Sunday)

Dark night of the soul, they call it—spiritual despair. Most of us go through it some time or another. Some live in that dark night for weeks, months, even years. In the early church they connected this kind of despair with the deadly sin of sloth. Sloth at that time meant more or less just sinking into a blue funk and saying the heck with the whole business. One writer called it "the refusal of joy."

It's weird, isn't it, that so few Christians have any joy. We call the story of Jesus the gospel, a word that means "good news," and yet so many Christian people live their lives as if it were *bad* news. It's crazy really. Why should someone by grumpy about good news? Why go around feeling like a worm?

Every so often on TV you see a savior and a saved person being interviewed. It may be a fireman who went into a burning house and pulled out a kid, or it may be a passing motorist who dived into a river and got someone out of a submerged car, or it may be a mountain climber who rescued a skier trapped on a ledge.

Both savior and saved are interviewed. The savior is usually modest about his or her bravery or heroism. The saved is almost always thankful to be alive—and happy, and looks at the savior with earnest eyes that silently shout, "I'm sure glad you showed up when you did."

If you and I could look Jesus in the eye like that, if we could see him really dying on the cross, if there were soldiers holding us by both arms because we too were accused and condemned—and if the minute Jesus died, they let us go and said, "You're free now," wouldn't we scream for joy? Wouldn't we run up and shout, even to our Savior's broken body on the cross, "Thank you!" Tears would stream down our cheeks, tears of thankfulness and joy. "Thank you."   SS

For Your Tears Jesus Died (Monday)

"My God, my God, why have you forsaken me?"
(Ps. 22:1).

As he agonized on the cross, why didn't Jesus quote
words of comfort, such as "Even though I walk through
the valley of the shadow of death, . . . you are with me"
(Ps. 23:4), instead of words of sorrow and loneliness,
"My God, my God, why have you forsaken me" (Ps.
22:1)? Jesus may have felt that he was utterly alone in
his pain, that God had left him.

With his cry, "Father, have you forgotten me?" Jesus
took all the swords of the world's pain, and gathering
them into one, pressed them into his own heart. When
you cry in sorrow and pain, Jesus has first felt your tears
on his own face as he died for you—your sorrow and
sins—on the cross.   KL

Expect a Miracle (Tuesday)

"Why are you so far from saving me. . .? I cry. . . but
you do not answer" (Ps. 22:1-2).

What is a miracle? It is hope in God that has come
alive through faith. A coincidence can also be a miracle,
God working anonymously.

I have a card that says: EXPECT A MIRACLE. GOD
IS ON YOUR SIDE. "The Bible tells us that if we
expect great things from God, great things will come to
pass," said a great preacher.

Although it is discouraging to receive no immediate
answer to prayer, it is important to expect one. Expect a
miracle; it may be disguised as coincidence. Pray with an
open mind and an expectant attitude. The results may
pleasantly surprise you.   KL

It's Your Choice (Wednesday)

"In you our fathers trusted" (Ps. 22:4).

Abraham became the father of a great nation because he chose to sacrifice his son as God commanded. Abraham trusted God, and God rewarded him by sparing Isaac.

God also tells us what conduct he expects of us, yet he gives us freedom to decide what we do—on a date, while taking a test, while talking, while interacting with others. As we struggle against our sinful natures to make choices that please God, we become closer to him, trusting he knows what is best for us. We trust God also to forgive us as we repent of our mistakes.

God loves us enough to give us freedom. Let us love God enough to use our freedom to honor him.   KL

Why Do Bad Things Happen to Good People? (Thursday)

"All who see me mock me [saying], 'He trusts in the Lord; let the Lord rescue him' " (Ps. 22:7-8).

Why does God allow tragedy to come to his people? Perhaps God allows trouble in life to remind us that we need him to govern, comfort, and protect us. When life is fine, we tend to forget about God. During times of trouble we return to God for help; nothing improves prayer life faster than big trouble.

Our faith in God and in ourselves is renewed in times of trouble. We realize we can overcome problems with the strength and comfort God provides.

The Lord *will* rescue his people from all trouble, for Jesus has promised, "Come to me, all who are weary and burdened, and I will give you rest" (Matt. 11:28).   KL

The Strategy of General Lee (Friday)

"Roaring lions tearing their prey open their mouths wide against me" (Ps. 22:13).

A visitor once asked Robert E. Lee what he thought of a certain individual. "He's a very fine gentleman," Lee replied.

"He says some very uncomplimentary things about you. What do you think about that?"

"You didn't ask me what he thought of me. You asked me what I thought of him."

The great Confederate general knew that Jesus commanded "Love your enemies" (Matt. 5:44). The general abided by one of the Lord's greatest strategies—a strategy for peace in one's heart that can bring peace to the world.   KL

Faith—the Wondrous Link (Saturday)

"Future generations will be told about the Lord" (Ps. 22:30).

Many faiths begin vicariously. Perhaps you learned of Jesus' love by listening to your parents or someone else pray, sing, and talk of their faith. Gradually, their faith became part of you.

Faith truly becomes your own when a personal relationship with God develops. This may take years of questioning, breaking away, and returning again to faith. Faith is a lifelong discovery of God's unwavering friendship.

As you live and grow in faith, your life becomes an example and an inspiration for others, the strengthening of one faith frequently strengthens another. Thus, faith is a wondrous link, not only between God and you, but also between you and those your life influences.   KL

Week 16   Matthew 27:11-31
Taking Good Advice (Sunday)

Pilate didn't take her advice. Sure, he washed his hands of the whole affair and pretended he wasn't responsible, but he was. His wife warned him. She had a hunch. It was more than a hunch; it was a dream, a nightmare. "Don't have anything to do with that innocent man," she warned him.

Because he didn't take her advice, because he allowed a mob to have its way and ordered an innocent man to be executed, Pilate's name is on the lips of Christians in churches all around the earth. We stand up and confess our faith. We say, "He suffered under Pontius Pilate." It is said millions of times a week. What a way to be remembered.

Pilate's name is mud, forever, because he didn't know good advice when he heard it. He didn't listen to his wife. Most of you reading this aren't married, but you do have concerned friends, you do have parents, you do have teachers and pastors and neighbors.

I'll grant you that some people are too full of advice. I had a guy once try to teach me the "proper" way to squeeze a toothpaste tube. So what? Who cares? What difference does it make?

But some of our decisions are far more important than whether we hold a toothpaste tube upside down or right side up. There are people who *can* help us with our important decisions. We can ask their advice; we can listen to what they say; we can see if it makes sense— and if it does, we can take that advice, and act on it.

Pilate didn't. His name is mud forever. We wouldn't want that to happen to us, now would we?   SS

Banner of Faith (Monday)

"He gave no answer" (Matt. 27:12).

I know a man who, though unlike Jesus in most ways, was similar in that he liked to keep his secrets to himself. His mind was like an ocean—apparently clear and blue and mild, but powerful and deep.

"He gave no answer," said Matthew. While Jesus knew his own power, he did not reveal that knowledge to the chief priests. And, like the chief priests, we do not fully know Jesus' mind. That does not matter. What matters is that we learn to love him, and follow him. With our banner of faith flying before us, we follow the leader, whose mind we cannot fully know. All we need to know is love. DW

Modern Persuasions (Tuesday)

"But the chief priests and elders persuaded the crowd to ask for Barabbas" (Matt. 27:20).

There are many "chief priests and elders" in our lives, many things that persuade us to choose something less than Jesus: the friends who laugh at people who practice Christianity, activities that take us away from church, our own minds urging us to do things we know are wrong.

But it is dangerous to put anything else in Jesus' place. Nothing can take his place in our lives. Let's not let ourselves be persuaded to choose anything else! DW

A Punishment for Freedom (Wednesday)

"Why? What crime has he committed?" (Matt. 27:23).

Jesus had done no evil. He was innocent of any crime.
Yet he was persecuted. It seems unfair. What possible
reason could there be for his death?

God knows the answer to that question. I can only
guess at the answer, repeating what has been said for ages
and ages. Jesus' life was taken so that our lives might be
saved.

"That's silly," you might say, "I'm alive. See? I can
move my fingers, breathe, and so on." But all of us will
one day die, and even now so many things keep dragging
us down.

Jesus died—he fell down so that we might be lifted up,
now and forever.   DW

Turning Point (Thursday)

"Then the governor's soldiers took Jesus into the
Praetorium and gathered the whole company of soldiers
around him" (Matt. 27:27).

Sometime or another you may have felt like Jesus must
have felt. Sometime or another you may have felt as if
you were surrounded by an entire army of tyrants and
bullies.

You may have been taught Jesus' command to "turn
the other cheek" when someone is being mean to you.
This is a hard thing to do. But like Jesus, we can rise
above the pain others give us. Jesus had God by his side,
to help him. Likewise, God will help us ignore the
people who harm us. Remember God, and remember
that he is helping us to turn the other cheek.   DW

The Seen and the Real (Friday)

"They put a staff in his right hand and knelt in front of him and mocked him" (Matt. 27:29).

I believe there are at least two levels of understanding in any situation: there is what you see, and there is something else that is not so clearly visible. There is what is real.

The soldiers who took Jesus away to be crucified saw only with their eyes, not their hearts. They gave Jesus a scarlet robe to wear. They put a crown of thorns on his head. When he was clothed in his "royal" garb, they proceeded to mock him.

God gives us the ability to see beyond our eyes. When we do, the king's true colors shine through that ragged cloth he wore. His crown is truly royal. We can see his holiness. Jesus is indeed Lord.   DW

We Know (Saturday)

"Then they led him away to crucify him" (Matt. 27:31).

I read this verse, and it made me sit back in my chair a while. I thought of times long past. I thought of what a poor follower of Jesus might have felt as he or she saw Jesus being taken away. *Who do they think they are, anyway? That's my Jesus they're taking! They can't do this! I've got to stop them. But the guards. What can I do? Now they've taken him away.*

Jesus' disciples were helpless as they watched the crucifixion. There was nothing to console them. They didn't know there was a purpose for Jesus' death. They did not know that his death would bring new life to all people. In that we are lucky, for we know.   DW

Week 17   Luke 24:13-35

In the Breaking of Bread (Sunday)

What always got me about the road to Emmaus story was how long Cleopas and his friend walked and talked with Jesus and didn't recognize him. Maybe that happens to all of us sometimes, especially those times when we feel pretty much bummed out about the whole religion thing. During those times we think we have left Jesus behind, but he is there walking with us just the same.

Sometimes Jesus is in disguise. Sometimes he looks just like my best friend, or sometimes like my basketball coach, or sometimes like the man who runs the corner store. Jesus is often there, talking to us, and we don't recognize him.

Another thing that strikes me about the Emmaus story is what they were doing when they *did* recognize Jesus. They were eating. Doesn't sitting down to a meal together bring out the truth about us?

Let's say you and your mom are in the middle of a week-long war. You have had skirmish after skirmish. You can't seem to resolve your differences. And let's say grandma invites the whole family over for Sunday dinner. If your grandma is like most grandmas, you won't be far into the salad course before she asks, "What's wrong?" You can't sit at the table with someone for long before a relationship is revealed.

In the Emmaus text it says of Jesus, "He was recognized by them when he broke the bread." Mealtimes are times to know one another. They are times to rebuild bridges, to talk out problems, to deepen relationships.

Maybe that's why the Lord's Supper is so special. Jesus is known to us—and we are known to him—in the breaking of bread.   SS

In Sight, Faith (Monday)

"But they were kept from recognizing him" (Luke 24:16).

This verse took on new meaning the week I lost my glasses. I didn't recognize anyone! But the week taught me a lot about faith.

I realized how much my glasses are like my faith. Without them I stumble around in an out-of-focus world. I run into walls and fall down.

As I grow older, both forms of help grow stronger, and I depend on them more. I thought I had reached a point in my faith where it could grow no more. I was wrong. Each time I feel my faith is established, I learn something, or meet somebody, or go somewhere that sets me growing even more. There is no upper limit on the strength of faith. SD

Crucify Me? (Tuesday)

"About Jesus of Nazareth. . . . He was a prophet, powerful in word and deed before God and all the people" (Luke 24:19).

Lord, you stood up for what you believed. I know you want that of me, but do you know what you're asking? I can't just go around telling others about you! My voice is shaky and my vocabulary is small. I wouldn't know what to say. No one would believe me anyway.

And my friends! Can you imagine what they'd think of me if I started to live what I believe? They'd think I'd gone nutso, Lord! Why, they'd crucify me!

Crucify me? Crucify me. I get the point. But are you sure you want *me?* OK, Lord, you win, I'll try. SD

Count on Christ (Wednesday)

"We had hoped that he was the one who was going to redeem Israel" (Luke 24:21).

Paula was an angry person. She was angry at life for treating her so badly. She was angry at her parents for getting divorced. She was angry at Christ for letting her down. She had tried to end her anger by ending her life, but she felt Christ hadn't let her even succeed at this.

Many people feel let down by Christ at times. Two men on the road to Emmaus were sure they had been let down too. But like Paula, they were expecting the wrong thing. Christ can see our lives in a much greater perspective than we can, so even when we're sure of what we want, we can trust Christ to do what's best for us.   SD

Celebrating Life (Thursday)

"Did not the Christ have to suffer these things and then enter his glory?" (Luke 24:26).

I sat in the crowded church for the funeral service of one of my favorite teachers. There were so many reasons for sadness. She was a much-loved person. She had three beautiful children. She had died the slow painful death of cancer.

But instead of sorrow, this service was a celebration! There were no dark "funeral" remarks or mournful hymns. The entire service was a celebration of life. She wanted it that way. She had written the service herself.

Christ has made it possible for everyone to feel this celebration of life in death. Because Christ suffered for us, we don't have to fear death. And because of that, we can live our lives more fully.   SD

Prayer Bread (Friday)

"When he was at the table with them, he took bread, gave thanks and broke it" (Luke 24:30).

The feeble knock at my front door snapped me out of my daydreaming. I opened the door to find Tillie, my elderly neighbor, standing there with a loaf of homemade bread. She handed it to me and explained, "This is very special bread. I know things have been hard for you lately, so I made you this prayer bread. The whole time I mixed, kneaded, and baked it, I prayed for you." And with that simple statement, she turned and left.

Jesus doesn't have to sit at our dining room tables to bless us. He comes to us every day in some of the most everyday things and people, and the blessings are just as wonderful.   SD

Quiet Examples (Saturday)

"Were not our hearts burning within us while he talked with us on the road. . .?" (Luke 24:32).

There were tears in my eyes as I hugged him once more before saying a final goodbye. We had only known each other for a very short time, but we had a special friendship. Beyond all our teasing, I saw in him a person I respected. Something about him stated clearly, "I'm a Christian." He doesn't know it, but I found strength and courage in his quiet example. I hope others can see that in me.

Jesus doesn't appear on too many roads anymore, but he is present in us and in people around us. He has surrounded us with people in whom we can see his quiet example, and he has put us here to be quiet examples for others.   SD

Week 18 Psalm 118
Where Trust Is Kept (Sunday)

Ann lay on the bed. Tears formed in the corners of her eyes. "I never should have trusted Sue," she said out loud.

It all started with a crush Ann had on Karl in the spring. Karl really didn't notice. He didn't pick up Ann's signals at all. She tried to be around places where she knew he'd show up—near his locker before school and after, and one table away from where he usually sat with his friends in the lunchroom. Nothing seemed to work.

About a week before school was out, Ann talked to Sue about her crush. It was supposed to be confidential. Ann thought it *was* confidential. Maybe Sue did too. But later she must have thought it would help to get something going if she told Karl about Ann's feelings.

The report came back to Ann from someone else. It was one of those "he said/she said," reports of a conversation. It may have been a fairly accurate report, but that didn't make Ann feel any better. When the reporter got to the part about Karl's reaction to the news of her interest, her "love" (if it was that), Karl laughed.

Maybe it would have been different if Karl had called and asked her for a date. Maybe then she would have thanked Sue for spilling the radishes. But Karl had laughed. He took her affection as a joke. How could he? How could she? How could they?

Ann would rebuild her friendship with Sue in time. By next fall she would even be able to face Karl without blushing. But a small crack was made in the foundation of her trust in other people. She would put her trust in God always, but she would be a bit more careful about how she trusted other people.   SS

Thank You (Monday)

"Give thanks to the Lord, for he is good; his love endures forever" (Ps. 118:1).

"Thank you" is a very simple phrase in which we express our appreciation to one another. A grocery cashier thanks the customers. A student thanks his friend for tutoring. An employee thanks her boss for a raise.

Yet, while we may remember to thank people, we often forget to appreciate what God has done for this world. As we look around us, we see many things to be thankful for: a home, parents, food, clothes, water, light. What's more, God's constant love is not only given to us through physical needs. God also gave us his only Son, who died on the cross to bring salvation to all human beings.

Have you said "thank you" to the Lord today?　　THP

Comfort for Sorrow (Tuesday)

"In my anguish I cried to the Lord, and he answered by setting me free" (Ps. 118:5).

My mother's brother was killed in a helicopter explosion in Vietnam. After his death, she used to kneel in front of our home altar for 10 or 15 minutes a day, murmuring to herself.

I asked my mother, "What are you doing at the altar?"

"Oh, just praying, child," she replied. "When I feel sorrowful I often pray and ask for God's comfort."

"Does God listen to you?"

"Yes, and God answers my prayers too."

"Really? How do you know that?"

"Very simple, my child," she said, taking me onto her lap. "You're a great comfort—from God to me."　　THP

On the Lord's Side (Wednesday)

"The Lord is with me; I will not be afraid" (Ps. 118:6).

Megan felt like the bottom had dropped out of her life. Everything seemed to be going wrong since she had lost her job. The situation became worse when she started drinking. Her friends tried to avoid her, and her family was embarrassed.

Megan had no one to talk to except Pastor Nelson. "Prayer," he said, "is the strongest weapon you can use now. God will listen to you, and he is on your side."

Megan trusted Pastor Nelson and took his advice. Every night, she prayed to God to give her confidence and strength to overcome her problems. Sometimes it takes a lot of time and help to straighten out our lives. But we can believe that God will strengthen and help us through prayer.   THP

Confidence in the Lord (Thursday)

"It is better to take refuge in the Lord than to trust in princes" (Ps. 118:9).

Our country, being a democracy, holds regular elections. After each one, we expect the newly elected officials to do their best to improve the situation for all people in our country.

While we trust and put confidence in our leaders, we often forget or ignore one very great influence—our Lord God. God has helped us and satisfied our needs since the world was first created. God has also shared our joy and pain through many generations. Presidents, prime ministers, kings, and princes have limited power. Many times, they fail in their promises to us. But God will never fail us, because God is the omnipotent one, King of kings and Lord of lords.   THP

The Gates (Friday)

"This is the gate of the Lord through which the righteous may enter" (Ps. 118:20).

The county fair's main gate was closed earlier than usual because the parking lots were filled. While I talked to my friends who worked there, some people came up to us and asked angrily, "Why did you guys close that gate? Getting through your stupid gate seems harder than going through the gate of heaven."

I knew they didn't mean it, but their statement made me think. The fair's gate was opened to all kinds of people; so is the gate of the Lord. The people had to pay their own money to enter the fair's gate, but the fee for the Lord's gate has already been paid by Jesus Christ.

THP

Light and Darkness (Saturday)

"The Lord is God, and he has made his light shine upon us" (Ps. 118:27).

As a child, I was always afraid of darkness. Especially at night, when the light suddenly went out, I often found myself staring at the surrounding shadows and imagining creepy things. It was even worse when I got up to search for a flashlight. I kept stubbing my toes against the tables and stumbling against the doors.

In the same way, without God, I find myself surrounded by the darkness of sin with no way out. Like the flashlight, God not only shows me where to go but also gives me comfort and confidence. God's love and guidance are our spiritual lights. "The Lord is God, and he has made his light shine upon us."   THP

Week 19   Exodus 15
A Different Victory (Sunday)

Victory is something to sing about. Moses had taken
God at his word and had set out toward the wilderness.
The victory over the pursuing armies of Pharaoh was just
the first and most obvious of many victories. Later on
there would be victories over idolatry (the golden calf),
ungratefulness (the manna), and grumbling (the water
rock).

When it comes to ungratefulness, we know where God
stands. When we are showered with blessing on
blessing—food in abundance, beautiful clothing, warm
homes—and then we gripe and complain because mom
and dad won't give us our own telephones or our own
cars, we know where God stands.

Half the world is in poverty. Hundreds of people starve
each day. How can I grumble and complain?

When it comes to idolatry, we know where God
stands. "You shall have no other gods before me," he
says, but I set myself up as a rival. I worship *me*
sometimes—and if not me, then my boyfriend or
girlfriend—or even some *thing,* like money or clothes or
sound equipment—or even a non-thing like popularity,
like being well-known or well-liked, like getting good
grades.

Victories are still won over these things. We pray for
help. Help comes. Our attitudes change and our actions
change. We call that a victory. Then, like Moses, we
chant: "I will sing to the Lord, for he is highly exalted."

SS

Escape Routes (Monday)

"The Lord is my strength and my song" (Exod. 15:2).

"Do you ever get depressed and not know why?"
Wendy asked.

Shelley nodded. "And then I imagine all sorts of
horrible tragedies, none my fault, in which I suddenly get
sick or hurt."

"I do that too! I even imagine dying."

"Life just seems so impossibly difficult sometimes. I
guess we want to escape."

"So what do you do to get out of that mood?"

"I sing. I don't always solve anything, but I feel
better—especially if I've been singing about God's power
and love, because I remember that God is always with
me. Life isn't impossible then."   PAF

The Right Perspective (Tuesday)

"Who among the gods is like you, O Lord? Who is like
you—majestic in holiness. . .?" (Exod. 15:11).

He said he'd call. He didn't. When I called, the
phone was busy. As usual.

The song in Exodus 15 begins, "I will sing to the
Lord." Why? What has God done for me? I guess since
I'm not the Hebrew nation, God won't part any seas for
me.

But I can't stay in this mood. I don't like bitterness,
and eventually I remember that even if Chet always
called, even if he fulfilled all my dreams, God is better
still. The Lord made me to be happiest with him.
Majestic in holiness Chet is not. I do care about Chet,
but I don't need to be desperate!   PAF

Confusion (Wednesday)

"Who is like you. . .awesome in glory, working wonders?" (Exod. 15:11).

This whole biblical song bothers me. How can glorious deeds be awesome? God is for peace, yet won a victory in war. God saved Israel with the Red Sea, but killed the Egyptians with it. God is supposed to be loving, but consumed people in his fury. I don't think I like that. Is God good?

Wait! Maybe God's deeds are called awesome because they're just *so good.* God *is* fighting a war, a war against evil. And when it's over, there really will be peace. Besides, God doesn't want to destroy anyone—he did send Jesus Christ to die and rise again to *save* us. So God is good! PAF

Celebration of Here (Thursday)

"In your strength you will guide them to your holy dwelling" (Exod. 15:13).

I sing praises to my God. The words don't always make sense, but it doesn't matter. God knows what they mean, and I am singing out of love.

I sing because God has brought me to this point in our relationship—even though I know our relationship has to go deeper still. The majestic God has fought many enemies to bring us close. My biggest enemy seems to be laziness, not vengeance.

I am *here now,* and that is good. Tomorrow the Holy One will lead me further. I am content. God loves me and can be trusted. So I sing. PAF

Adamless (Friday)

"So the people grumbled against Moses, saying, 'What are we to drink?' " (Exod. 15:24).

Holy God, do you give hugs? I need one tonight. This world is so frustrating. I thirst for a hug from one who feels my darkness. I think I'll let go of my sanity if my need isn't met.

No hugs? No hugs? I'm lonely, Lord! Please, before the blackness crushes my eyes!

No hugs.

They must come by transfer. Who shall be my connection? Eve had Adam. Where's my Adam?

And you say, "No Adam. Not yet."

Shall I live?

So you send my mother. She does not understand my darkness, yet her hug comforts.

"I am the Lord, your God," you thunder.   PAF

Hope versus Despair (Saturday)

"I am the Lord who heals you" (Exod. 15:26).

I had no energy. But while I was looking for physical diseases, God pointed at my soul. I was afraid to look there until someone finally asked, "Have you considered seeing a psychologist?"

I was embarrassed, but I went to one. She was a Christian, and she uncovered a fierce battle in me: hope versus despair.

"What's this despair?" God asked. "Don't you know me?"

Despair and lack of energy creep back every now and then, but God showed me that there is no reason to despair. Someday I'll be all hope and dancing!   PAF

Week 20 Genesis 8:13-22; 9:8-17
God's Remnant (Sunday)

Again and again in the Bible God used a remnant to continue his plans. A seamstress might think we were talking about a scrap of cloth, but we are talking about scraps of people—small handfuls left over after a war, a catastrophe, or a period of unfaithfulness.

The story of Noah is the tale of a remnant. The story tells of the wholesale destruction of humankind in a flood, but God saved a handful to carry on his creation. Noah and his family were that handful.

If you are a believer in Christ, you may at times have felt like a remnant. Maybe almost everyone in your class was thinking or acting one way—and you thought and maybe acted another. It was because of your beliefs. You didn't go on the outing. You stayed home from the party. You were the only one in your whole class who wouldn't contribute to a fund to hire a streaker to run across the football field during graduation exercises.

Remnants don't have it that easy. You can bet that Noah was ridiculed and teased by his neighbors for building his silly boat on dry land.

But remnants often have the last laugh. Mostly they don't laugh, though. Like Darlene, who didn't go to the party because she knew there'd be heavy drinking. And there was an accident. One of her friends was killed and another paralyzed for life.

Or Pete, who saw that their Halloween pranks were turning into vandalism. He left his friends and went elsewhere. He didn't laugh when the others were caught, convicted, fined, and put on probation.

God uses remnants to carry on his truth, to witness to the world, and sometimes to *avert* catastrophe. Maybe you are a part of one of those remnants. If so, you are cut from some pretty good cloth.   SS

A Little Prayer (Monday)

"Then Noah built an altar to the Lord" (Gen. 8:20).

My grandmother recently made it through a rough illness. Without realizing it I repeated a saying that has been around for years. It is a little prayer that is either spoken or shown through the actions of somebody who has had a worry lifted from their shoulders.

Noah showed his thanks by building an altar; I showed my thanks through a little prayer, two small words: *Thank God!*   TLM

The Gift of Seasons (Tuesday)

"As long as the earth endures. . .summer and winter. . .shall not cease" (Gen. 8:22).

When I sit outside and see all that God has given us—the plants, the trees, sun, and even summer—I realize how lucky we are.

God made us all a promise. God said that as long as the earth remains, summer and winter will not end. God is showing his love for us through the regularity of the seasons. As God's love will always be there, so will the change of the seasons.

So, on the darkest day of winter when the sun is hidden by a blanket of clouds, remember that summer will soon be here, and that God is always here.   TLM

God Won't Give Up on Us (Wednesday)

"Never again will there be a flood to destroy the earth" (Gen. 9:11).

God is more patient than we are. In the time of Noah, almost everyone had forgotten God; yet God spared the few who hadn't forgotten him. God didn't give up on them.

In our own time, God forgives us and gives us a second chance.

God hasn't given up on us yet, and for the sake of Jesus, God never will!   TLM

A Sign of Comfort (Thursday)

". . . a covenant for all generations to come" (Gen. 9:12).

When God made a covenant with Noah years ago, he was thinking of us, too, the generations to come.

Even today, after a bad storm God places the rainbow in the clouds to remind us (and himself!) of the promises he made.

After covering the earth with water, God sent the rainbow as a sign to us that there was hope for the future.

I have a picture of a rainbow in my room, I look at that picture and remember that there is hope for the future. God sent the rainbow as a sign of comfort for all generations to come.   TLM

I Remember the Promise (Friday)

"Whenever the rainbow appears in the clouds, I will see it and remember" (Gen. 9:16).

When the rainbow appears in the clouds. . .
   I will remember how once people were so evil
   God destroyed the earth.
When the rainbow appears in the clouds. . .
   I remember Noah, so full of love for God,
   his life was spared.
When the rainbow appears in the clouds. . .
   I remember the dove, who brought a leaf and hope.
When the rainbow appears in the clouds. . .
   I remember Noah's offering of thanks.
When the rainbow appears in the clouds. . .
   I remember the promise.   TLM

Calm after the Storm (Saturday)

"This is the sign of the covenant I have established between me and all life on the earth" (Gen. 9:17).

   It came quick, hit hard, and left suddenly, destroying some of the garages in the area.

   As I walked around the neighborhood, I realized how peaceful everything seemed after the storm. The rays of sun filtering through the clouds were so beautiful you wouldn't believe how strong the previous storm was.

   Then I saw it, God's promise that the storm was over and everything would be all right. That beautiful rainbow was God telling me not to worry.   TLM

Week 21   Genesis 11:1-9

One Language and a Few Words (Sunday)

Wouldn't life be simple if there were one language and few words? Just think of how much easier international relations would be if Russians, Chinese, Americans, Africans and all the rest could communicate in one simple language.

There *is* one language, a universal language, that speaks to all people everywhere—the language of love. Often it uses no words at all. Love speaks out in action.

How many books have you read by Mother Teresa? How many speeches have you heard her make on TV? How often is she quoted in the news? She won the Nobel Prize writing no words at all and speaking few. Her ministry is to the dying poor. She simply acts out Christ's love to those least likely to get any from elsewhere.

Actions *do* speak louder than words—and when we do speak up, all too often the words get us into trouble. James, Chapter 3, talks about that. The tongue, it says, is a fire, a restless evil, full of deadly poison.

We jokingly use phrases like "Bite my tongue," "Wash out my mouth," or "Shame on me" when we have said something unkind, thoughtless, or gossipy. How many times do we say to ourselves, "Oh, I wish I had never said that." And when we write down our vile and foul and angry words, it seems even worse. Angry words that are spoken, sort of fade into the air after a time. When they're written down, they are just as harsh and cruel and awful every time someone pulls them out and rereads them.

Maybe the Tower of Babel story, describing as it does the confusion of human languages, is a reminder to us that language is always second best. The good that we try to do for others is almost always better done with actions than with words.   SS

He Has Scattered the Proud (Monday)

"Come, let us build ourselves a city" (Gen. 11:4).

Bill had just received an A on a term paper. His baseball team finished first in the league, and he had won the batting title. To top it all off, he had just learned that his graduation gift was to be a new car. He began to brag of his achievements. In fact, he became so self-centered and arrogant that others began avoiding him. Bill's bragging, instead of helping him, worked against him.

The people of Shinar too were filled with pride. But it led to their downfall. We don't need to brag about our accomplishments to find status and security. We have that in Jesus, who loved us all the way to the cross.   PJR

What's in a Name? (Tuesday)

"Come, . . . make a name for ourselves. . ." (Gen. 11:4).

"He's a big name in show business." "She's a big name in literature." Have you ever heard anyone say that? To be a "big name" means that a person stands out above all the rest. People work hard to become "big names." The people in ancient Babel certainly did.

However, we need to remember that being a "big name" counts for nothing in God's sight. What counts is that we confess *the* name which is above every name, the name of our Lord Jesus Christ. Baptized into *his* name, we are forgiven and accepted by God. Then we are sent out to love and serve others in the name of Jesus. That is the name we bear (*Christ*-ian!). That is the name we share.   PJR

A Name for Ourselves (Wednesday)

". . . so that we may make a name for ourselves" (Gen. 11:4).

We try so hard to make a name for ourselves. The people in the land of Shinar did also. They built a tall tower that would reach to the heavens. They wanted to be known and remembered forever.

We too want to be known and remembered. Some aspire to be rock stars or political figures or great scientists, in order that they may be remembered long after death.

However, we need to remember that being remembered by God is the most important thing. The highest status one can have is to be God's child. In our Baptism God called us by name. We are his. God will never forget our names.   PJR

For Ourselves (Thursday)

". . . so that we may make a name for ourselves (Gen. 11:4).

"Honey, the boss just gave me a big raise! Now we can finally get a new car and a decent stereo!"

"That's wonderful, dear, but shouldn't we think of others as well as ourselves?"

"Oh, come on, for once let's think about ourselves and what we want. Didn't you want a microwave?"

"It would be nice, dear, but our stove works just fine. Let's not spend it all on things for ourselves. We only gave $5 to the United Way, and I turned down the lady from the Cancer Society. And our church offerings! Wouldn't God want us to think more about others and less about things?"

"You're right, honey. When you stop to think of it, we have so much. Let's share it."   PJR

Babel and Babble (Friday)

"Let us go down and confuse their language" (Gen. 11:7).

We might say that at Babel people began to babble! The *American Heritage Dictionary* defines *babble*: "to utter incoherent, meaningless sound." That is what happened long ago in Babel. Because of their pride the Lord confused their language. Prideful talk is really "babble," isn't it? One keeps on telling how great one is or how much one has accomplished.

God was displeased with the pride of the people of Babel, just as he is displeased with our reliance on our own works for our worth. Let us count instead on Christ's accomplishments for us—his death and resurrection. There we have the status and security of God's forgiven children. PJR

One Another's Speech (Saturday)

"There the Lord confused the language of the whole world" (Gen. 11:9).

Long ago God confused the language of the people of Babel because of their pride. That was an act of judgment. But God also acted in mercy. Thousands of years later he cleared up the confusion of Babel—at Pentecost in Jerusalem. "All of them were filled with the Holy Spirit and began to speak in other tongues" (Acts 2:4).

What happened at Pentecost was therefore the opposite of what happened at Babel. The disciples proclaimed the good news of Jesus, and people from all over the world heard the gospel "in their own languages." Judgment was replaced by grace! PJR

Week 22   Acts 2:1-42
Babel Revisited (Sunday)

What happened to God's people at the Tower of Babel
was suddenly and miraculously—though momentarily—
restored on the Day of Pentecost: God gave the gift of
other tongues. Simple fishermen like Peter and Andrew,
James and John were suddenly and without study or
training able to preach the good news of Jesus in other
languages.

Just suppose a dozen members of a youth group went to
meet their leader returning from a conference. They are
in the middle of a crowd at international airport when
God zaps them. Suddenly John, the all-conference
tackle, is speaking Swahili, and Frances, the soloist, is
speaking Pakistani, and Martha has a crowd of Russian
diplomats standing around her.

That's the story of Pentecost. Unlearned men were
speaking languages and dialects they had never studied.
The power of God was at work in the world.

Even though we mostly converse with those who speak
the same language, we are often misunderstood. You
don't need to cross any language barriers to be
understood. Just the way you say OK to your mom or dad
gets misinterpreted. Don't you wish someone would really
understand for once—I mean *really* understand?

Well, dearly bewildered, I have some wonderful news
for you. Jesus speaks your language—and hears it too.
Spill your whole story to him. He listens, and he
understands. You don't even have to say the words out
loud. Just think.

The miracle of letting Jesus understand you first is that
he helps you understand yourself too. That makes it
easier to talk to mom, dad, sis, brother, coach, teacher,
and all the rest. Neat, eh?   SS

The Descent of Direction (Monday)

"When the day of Pentecost came, they were all together in one place" (Acts 2:1).

Picture this: it's been nine days since Jesus ascended into heaven. The disciples are like scolded dogs—eager to please, a little hurt, and mostly confused. They have the difficult task of spreading God's Word. But they lack a leader. The big question is, "Are we on the right track?"

Right when the need is greatest, the Holy Spirit descends on the disciples. Direction is given, they have hope for their mission, and each is filled with the Holy Spirit.

Pentecost is important to us as well, for the hope and strength passed on by the Holy Spirit is present in us. The Holy Spirit descends in our prayers and clears the confusion around us. DW

The Turnaround (Tuesday)

"All of them were filled with the Holy Spirit" (Acts 2:4).

Sometimes you hear about somebody's life changing overnight. Maybe they almost died of a heart attack, so they turned around completely. Or maybe they read a book that really shook them up. They might have had to fight in a war, and they were never the same again.

Things like that can happen to you. Sometimes the changes are good, and sometimes they're lousy. Something happened to the disciples on the Day of Pentecost that turned their lives around. They stopped hiding out in upper rooms and started preaching about Jesus to everybody they saw.

When the Holy Spirit comes into the picture, things happen! DW

Our Own Tongues (Wednesday)

"We hear them declaring the wonders of God in our own tongues!" (Acts 2:11).

Ronnie hated trees. And flowers. In fact, Ronnie hated just about anything green. Ronnie's love was for the city.

Joe hated streets, tall buildings, and anything that wasn't meant to change but to last.

Ronnie hears the song of the street. He feels the life of the city pulsing beneath his tennis-shoed feet. Ronnie hears God in the city.

Joe hears the song of the wood. He feels the easy motion of the growing things, moving in and out and among each other. Joe hears a country God.

In our own ways, we hear God's mighty works.   DW

Fear and Love (Thursday)

"But God raised him from the dead, freeing him from the agony of death, because it was impossible for death to keep its hold on him" (Acts 2:24).

God raised Jesus from the dead. That one sentence says a mouthful.

The dead normally remain dead. This is a fact that does not have to be proved by our scientists.

Jesus was held dear to God—more dear than anything else on earth.

God is his own ruler. God makes the rules.

By this one simple, incredible act, we can see the awesome power of God and can love and fear him for it.

We can fear God for his power. We can love God for what he does with his power.   DW

Breakfast with Trep and Lenny (Friday)

"We are all witnesses" (Acts 2:32).

Trep woke up, stepped into his slippers, and went to the table. Lenny did the same. Trep and Lenny said good morning to each other. Then Trep said, "I'm going to eat my cereal now." Lenny didn't say anything, and started eating.

Witnessing faith is a lot like Trep and Lenny's breakfast. Some people declare their faith and tell everyone they meet about the glories and wonders of God. That's being a witness, and that's OK. Other people accept their faith, like Lenny accepting his cereal. That's OK, too.

Just as we all must eat, we all are witnesses. We all are witnesses of our faith in God.   DW

Repent and Be Baptized (Saturday)

"Repent and be baptized" (Acts 2:38).

I have felt the cries of the innocent and the cheated, and I plugged my senses. For this I repent. I have shown a friend a gift, then broken it over his doorstep. For this I repent. I have stacked one thoughtless word on top of another. For this I repent.

We can receive what Christ has freely given. He has opened what once was closed. He has traveled to the Father and sent us his Spirit. In his name we have been baptized.   DW

Week 23   Psalm 16
In Pleasant Places (Sunday)

It's count your blessings time. The psalmist wrote, "The boundary lines have fallen for me in pleasant places." He must have been talking about how God had blessed him, how the boundaries of his life had been laid out quite wonderfully.

It may be a little harder for you to count blessings before much of your life has been lived. You can't look back and say, "Well, I came from a pretty obscure hometown and am the product of a broken marriage and went to a wimpy little college, but now I'm a manager— or a pilot or an architect or an opera singer or a pastor."

But you *have* lived enough of life to know you are blessed in some special ways:

1. You were born in and/or live in "the land of the free." Think about that.
2. You have some friends, maybe not hundreds of them, but they are very special. Form their names on your lips.
3. You have a lot of people who love you and care what happens to you. Stop a minute and count them on your fingers.
4. You are probably in pretty good health. Whisper the names of some diseases and disabilities among people you know that you *don't* have.
5. God loves you. God loves everybody.
6. You love God. Count the people you know who don't.

Have the lines fallen for you in pleasant places? Are you blessed? Should you be ashamed all the way down to your ingrown toenails for sometimes being ungrateful? Or dissatisfied? Or unfulfilled? Well, I guess.   SS

Alternatives (Monday)

"I said to the Lord, 'you are my Lord; apart from you I have no good thing' " (Ps. 16:2).

There is a place I stand when life is too hard for me. I call it the Edge. If I step over the Edge, I am stepping into madness. Wouldn't that be a good way out of everything? No more guilt, no more stress, no more responsibility. If I don't step over, I have to walk back into life. But why should I do that? Life is *hard!*

Then God says, "What are you doing? You know that I am with you. Yes, life is hard; I know. But it is good, because I am in it."

There is a power in holding back, but when pride crumbles, I climb into God's lap where I belong, saying, "I am lost without you."   PAF

Christian Friends (Tuesday)

"As for the saints who are in the land, they are the glorious ones, in whom is all my delight" (Ps. 16:3).

Before Leah had moved to town, Patti had been lonely at school. She had had friends, but they weren't Christians, so she couldn't share all her deepest dreams and thoughts with them. Many of those secrets were embedded in her Christianity, and she knew her friends wouldn't understand. But Leah was a Christian and had understood.

Leah had been so encouraging to her, reminding her of God's love when she was discouraged, sharing with Patti her understanding of God, and praying for her. Patti knew God was always with her, but it helped so much to have a Christian friend to remind her, someone she could see and touch.   PAF

Eternal Destiny (Wednesday)

"The sorrows of those will increase who run after other gods" (Ps. 16:4).

Tricia didn't have any close friends because she was always studying hard so she could become a doctor. But she was lonely. She didn't even have time for God. "I don't like this life," she finally admitted. "I'm living as if my grade-point average determined my eternal destiny. My relationship with God determines that! What have I been worshiping?"

And wasn't it ironic that she wanted to be a doctor but didn't have time for people? She needed to be a doctor whose job was part of her dedication to God, and because of God's love for people, also part of her dedication to people. She didn't have to be lonely.   PAF

Booming Book (Thursday)

"I will praise the Lord, who counsels me; even at night my heart instructs me" (Ps. 16:7).

I wish God would speak to me in a big booming voice and tell me what to do after I graduate. After all, he spoke to Moses and other people. Why can't God speak to me?

But Moses didn't have the Bible, and I do. That's God's big booming voice to me. God could literally speak to me if that were wisest. He hasn't, so I guess the Bible must be enough. And God has given me prayer and other Christians to help me, too. If I read one of the Gospels and prayerfully study Jesus, I'll see what is important to him, and that will be my big booming voice saying, "Do this!"   PAF

Mobility (Friday)

"I have set the Lord always before me. . . I will not be shaken" (Ps. 16:8).

It's true. When I'm regular about prayer and Bible study, I keep God before me, and I am not moved. Then I know exactly who I am—God's own child—and nothing can shake me.

It's also true, however, that it is hard to do that. I can't keep that up on my own for long. So I mustn't forget the Holy Spirit, God himself working in me, helping me to pray, helping me to read and understand, and helping me to know who I am. God loves me and delights in sending the Spirit to work in me.

With the Holy Spirit alive in me, who can shake me?

PAF

Fullness (Saturday)

"You have made known to me the path of life; you will fill me with joy in your presence" (Ps. 16:11).

Steve and I get along so great it is amazing. The only problem is that it's easy to forget God when I'm so happy with Steve. I forget that God has ordered our lives so that fullness of joy comes to us only in God's presence.

Steve brings me joy, but *fullness* of joy? God says that is what he wants for us. Fullness—overflowing with joy, stuffed with joy. How can we be content to settle for less? We can't seem to remember that fullness comes only from God, not from money, power, drugs, or sex. Even a relationship as great as Steve's and mine is just a *taste* of the fullness God has planned for us!   PAF

Week 24   Matthew 10:1-23
Give without Pay (Sunday)

When Jesus first sent his disciples out from town to town to preach the good news, he said, "You received without pay, give without pay." This was to be a volunteer mission. They were not to be paid religious professionals. They were to take with them no money, no extra clothes. They were advised to find the house of a worthy person in each town and to stay there while they taught and preached and healed.

Many of you who read this will come from the homes of volunteers. You may yourselves be volunteers. Consider that a blessing. Sure, volunteerism can be overdone. Occasionally a mom is so busy with her church work and her community-action projects and her library board and all, that she isn't around home much. Then it's hard not to be resentful.

But in healthy doses, volunteerism is an important, even essential, part of the Christian life. One marriage counselor recognizes in nearly every troubled marriage a kind of selfishness, an "everything for me" attitude. He often prescribes large doses of volunteer work to his troubled couples. He tries to get them to think about others rather than themselves.

That antidote works for teenagers too. If you are spending too much time thinking about yourself, how you look, how many friends you have, who you're going to sit with in the lunchroom, how likely you are to get a date for Thursday's game, maybe it's time to branch out.

Try the retirement center. Or how about the other end of the line: volunteer for the Sunday morning nursery in your church. There is plenty to do. Volunteer. It teaches you to be unselfish before you get too set in your ways. It may make for a happier marriage later on.

SS

Get Out Fast (Monday)

"If the home is deserving, let your peace rest on it; if it is not, let your peace return to you" (Matt. 10:13).

There are certain situations in which Christians should not place themselves. I knew I was in one and had to get out fast. I'd only come to the party because Stacey didn't want to go alone, but a lot of kids were drinking heavily and smoking—not regular cigarettes, either. Stacey was having fun and didn't want to leave even after I'd told her I was uncomfortable. Mom picked me up early.

Later, I heard the neighbors had called the police, and I was glad I hadn't been there. Sometimes, it's better to be your own person. My instincts told me this situation was not "deserving," and they were right. Maybe it wasn't just my instincts telling me something!   EMB

God Is Near (Tuesday)

"The kingdom of heaven is near" (Matt. 10:7).

"The kingdom of heaven is near." What does it mean? It was a warning to people to "shape up." God was near and judgment would follow.

But the kingdom of heaven is near is also a reassurance that God is near when we need him.

Both meanings are true. God is near—we'd better repent and watch our step. God is near—if we slip, he'll be there to help us out.   EMB

The Rock (Wednesday)

"Do not go among the Gentiles or enter any town of the Samaritans. Go rather to the lost sheep of Israel" (Matt. 10:5-6).

Lord, I'm troubled. If you really meant what you said about sending the disciples only to "the lost sheep of Israel," then I'm not saved, right? How do I figure that? Well, I'm a lost sheep, but not from Israel.

Hey, I just thought of something. There were a lot of people to tell the good news to, more people than disciples. But if *they* told the Gentiles, and the *Gentiles* told the Samaritans, and they *all* told—well, you get the idea. It would almost be like throwing a rock into a pond. You see, *you're* the rock, and you make ripples which make more ripples, and soon the whole pond is rippled. (That's because you're such a big, powerful rock!)   EMB

A Second Job (Thursday)

"It will not be you speaking, but the Spirit of your Father speaking through you" (Matt. 10:20).

Today's society offers us many career options: doctor, farmer, scientist, factory worker, homemaker, and on and on. It's hard to choose just one, but whatever we choose, we already have one full-time job. As children of God, we are all called to be disciples of Christ.

At first, this may not seem like a full-time job. Yet, at the same time as we work at our chosen occupation, we are also to work at telling others about God, spreading the good news in spite of our enemies. Just as a job at a supermarket, a bank, or a hospital will put physical food on the table, our job as a disciple of Jesus will put spiritual food on the table.   EMB

Discipling (Friday)

"All men will hate you because of me" (Matt. 10:22).

"So you want to be a disciple?"

"Yes, Lord!"

"Tell me, then, what does a disciple do?"

"Well, a disciple heals the sick, raises the dead, cleanses lepers, and casts out demons. A disciple is a wonderful person to be!"

"I see. Do you know that a disciple also gives without receiving, loves while others hate, and is persecuted by many? Disciples of mine have been killed because of me."

"They have?"

"Yes, child."

"Lord, I don't think I'm quite ready to be a disciple. Can I come back when I feel more prepared?"

"Yes, child. If it isn't too late."   EMB

A Lesson on Endurance (Saturday)

"But he who stands firm to the end will be saved" (Matt. 10:22).

There is a weeping willow tree in my backyard by the fields. My 12-year-old brother and his friend are now in the process of building a tree house, and this tree is the strongest and best in our yard for that purpose.

It wasn't always so. I can remember when a twig from my grandfather's willow was thrown at the edge of the field. It took root, choked off a lot of weeds, and grew to be a tall, sturdy tree.

To my brother, it's just a tree, perfect for summer pleasures. To me, who can remember what it was, it gives a message to stand firm. It wasn't always easy for this tree. The winter can be cruel, but this willow endured and was saved as we will be if, with God's help, we can only stand firm to the end.   EMB

Week 25   Luke 10:25-37
Loving the Loner (Sunday)

The story of the good Samaritan doesn't have the same punch today as it had when Jesus told it. When we hear it today, we can't really feel the profound differences between Jews and Samaritans. That anybody should go down in the ditch to help an injured person is remarkable; that a Samaritan would help a Jew is that much more remarkable.

Helping the helpless, befriending the friendless, looking after the lonely—these are not easy tasks. In high school it may seem nearly impossible to befriend a real loner. Do you go up to a person and say, "I see you have no friends. I'd like to be your friend." Not likely. Even if you tried, it wouldn't work.

Getting to know a loner takes a little research. You need, first of all, to find out what that person is interested in—auto repair, cooking, paleontology, antiques, horses. Then do a little research into that subject, just enough so you can ask a couple of half-intelligent questions. Then make your approach.

Really lonely people are sometimes on the verge of desperation. Most teen suicides happen among the very lonely—or those who are suddenly alone—say a boyfriend or girlfriend breaks it off or moves away, a best friend dies or is killed, parents are divorced. Such a person really needs a friend.

As Christians we ought to be sensitive to loneliness. We ought to develop a keen sense for it. You like the person, don't you, who senses your sour moods and tries to sweeten you out of them?

That's sometimes what it means to be a good Samaritan among your peers. Some people you see every day have taken real psychological beatings. They may not be bloody, but they do hurt. Sense that hurt. Be a neighbor.   SS

Tests (Monday)

"An expert in the law stood up to test Jesus" (Luke 10:25).

I closed my eyes and prayed hard, hoping that by some miracle my prayer might be answered, and the chemistry final in front of me might be consumed in flame. No such luck. It lay there on my desk. If only I had studied instead of watching TV! With each question I saw my scholarship chances weakening. Surely the Lord would help me through this! Jesus knew how important college was to me!

Because I failed the test, I thought the Lord had abandoned me that day. Yet I had learned something. Christ knows what it's like to be tested. He hasn't promised to take away our tests, but he has promised to go through them with us.   SD

Opening Doors (Tuesday)

"Love the Lord your God with all your heart and with all your soul and with all your strength and with all your mind" (Luke 10:27).

Sometimes my life is like being in a house in a storm. Through the storm I heard a persistent knock at my door. Reluctantly, I opened it. There was Christ, wanting to come in. I wasn't sure what it meant to open the door to Christ, but I was sick of being alone in this storm.

In the years that followed, I learned more about opening doors to Christ. He came into my bedroom, where I studied and dreamed. He came into my rec room, where I relaxed and entertained friends. Christ even helped me clean my closet, where I'd kept so many things hidden. He has become my life.   SD

Masks *(Wednesday)*

"Love your neighbor as yourself" (Luke 10:27).

Todd, the all-star athlete, had asked for my help on a speech. I decided to help him, because I knew if I didn't, he'd just get someone else to do it for him. As we worked together, I began to see beyond the macho mask Todd wore. Behind it there was a super person, one with an excellent sense of humor and a real talent for writing. I had unfairly judged Todd by the mask he wore.

Sometimes we put up fronts so well that no one looks behind them. We become the only one who really knows what's there. When someone seems to have no good points, it may only be that they are too well hidden. If you want others to look behind your mask, start by seeing past theirs. SD

Brains, Nerds, and Jocks *(Thursday)*

"But a Samaritan. . . took pity on him" (Luke 10:33).

Jenny is a brain. Tom is a nerd. Mark is a jock. These are the labels Jenny, Tom, and Mark are known by to the whole school. Very few people have taken the time to learn that Jenny really hates school, or that Tom has an excellent sense of humor, or that Mark is worried about getting into college.

Labels can be ugly things. They're like boxes that we put people into so we never have to deal with them. We all label others; it's a hard habit to kick. Jesus asks us to try and see people as he does, without the labels. Going beyond labels isn't easy. It means associating with the people in the ditches and seeing them as friends. SD

Alone (Friday)

"A Samaritan. . . went to him and bandaged his wounds" (Luke 10:33-34).

There once was a man who lived alone. He traveled often, but always alone. Whenever the people of his town saw him, he was alone. He had spent most of his life alone. He was very lonely.

One day he went for a walk. He was alone, of course. He saw a man lying in the ditch. The man who had lived most of his life alone saw a chance to be needed. He cared for the beaten man by pouring oil and wine on his wounds and leaving him at an inn. In all of his aloneness he had reached out to someone who needed him. Somehow he didn't feel quite so alone.   SD

Taking the Challenge (Saturday)

"Go and do likewise" (Luke 10:37).

I challenged myself to live the life of a good Samaritan. After a week's effort, I have learned many things. There is much more to Samaritan-ing than picking people out of gutters and getting them on their feet again. Before you can help someone out you have to step down into the gutter. Bandaging wounds won't heal a person completely. The story doesn't end at the inn. A Samaritan returns to pay the bills and thinks about and prays for the injured one. When at last the injured one is able to go on, the prayers don't stop. To be a Samaritan is to invest part of ourselves in each person we reach out to.   SD

Week 26   Psalm 139

Known of God (Sunday)

The psalmist wrote about knowledge. He was known by God. God knew his sitting down, his standing up, his insides and outsides. In older translations of the Bible the word *known* could mean sexual intercourse, the most intimate sharing of one's self with another: "Now Adam *knew* Eve his wife, and she conceived and bore Cain," or, "Rebekah was very fair to look upon, a virgin, whom no man had known."

The psalmist talked this way about God. He didn't see God in a sexual way, of course, but he recognized that God knew him better than a wife could, better than a mother. Indeed, God had knit him together in his mother's womb.

It is scary to be so well known, but it is freeing too. Most of us are best known in our own homes, and that's what makes home such a comfortable place. At home I am better known, more fully accepted than in any other place. I can be myself at home.

Just so with God. How can I hide from God? *What* can I hide from God? The psalmist said, "If I go up to the heavens, you are there; if I make my bed in the depths, you are there."

That is really a freeing realization. I can't hide from God, so why try? God already knows me better than I know myself, so why pretend? I am therefore at home with God. He knows my secret sins, my secret desires, my hopes, fears, apprehensions, dreams. God knows everything about me.

But the best part is that God doesn't laugh. He doesn't ridicule. God understands because Jesus has been here, and Jesus and God are one. We are understood, you and I, we are loved, and we will someday be judged by someone who has been through it all. We are known by God.   SS

The Mysterious One (Monday)

"Such knowledge is too wonderful for me, too lofty for me to attain" (Ps. 139:6).

The Lord is a mystery. I know nothing about God except his love for me and everyone else. The Lord knows so much about me, from the past to the future. Yet I know so little about him. Why does God keep himself so secret? I have many questions for him.

God's knowledge is so complex and great. I just can't understand it. But then, all I really have to know is that God knows everything about me and even so, he loves me completely.   AW

You Cannot Escape (Tuesday)

"If I go up to the heavens, you are there; if I make my bed in the depths, you are there" (Ps. 139:8).

"Boy, am I depressed. I'm flunking school already, and now my parents are getting depressed."

"Hey, Todd, forget that. I have some stuff that will make you feel great!"

Sad to say, this is a common situation for many young people who turn to drugs and begin to destroy their own lives.

I don't take drugs, because I think it is a waste and cheap way of escaping life's problems. Besides, when the drugs wear off, the problem is still there. Since you cannot escape either problems or God, why not turn to God for help with the problems? God cares!   AW

I'm Special (Wednesday)

"For you created my inmost being; you knit me together in my mother's womb" (Ps. 139:13).

"John, you're a born loser," said Tim.

"No, I'm not," said John. "I'm somebody special. God doesn't make junk!"

John is right. God makes every person special. God knows everything about you, even before you are born. God also shapes your future. God gives everyone not only love, but everything else they need.

How great to know that God made us and that we are God's main concern!   AW

I Have Doubts (Thursday)

"Search me, O God, and know my heart" (Ps. 139:23).

When my friend died from leukemia, I said to God, "I don't understand. You say that you will protect us, yet you let people die. Why?"

It's hard to help people to believe, because their doubts get in the way. They ask, "If God is so great, why are there tornadoes, earthquakes, wars, and deaths?"

It's hard to think of answers for them, because I am not sure myself. But I do know that God is with us always and will take care of us even when we die.

I pray, "God, I love you. Search me, know my heart, take my doubts, and lead me on."   AW

Problems and Solutions (Friday)

"Test me and know my anxious thoughts" (Ps. 139:23).

When I started high school, it was hard for me to choose which courses to take. I wanted to take many of the classes listed, but I couldn't take *all* of them. Which ones would be best for me? I had a problem.

We all have problems. Some are big and some are small. Writers get rich producing problem-solving books that are helpful to some of us, some of the time.

A book that can be helpful to all of us, all of the time, is the Bible. In it God speaks to us. God knows us and our thoughts. No problem is too big for God to care about and help us with.   AW

Guide Me (Saturday)

"See if there is any offensive way in me, and lead me in the way everlasting" (Ps. 139:24).

Our future can be scary but also challenging. It's scary because we don't know what will happen to us.

A friend of mine prayed, "Dear God, graduation is coming and I don't know what to do with my life. Help me! Lead me!"

My friend had the right idea. Rough times come for all of us, but through prayer we open ourselves up to God's correction and leading.

God knows where I need help and what is best for me. The Lord even knows what is still coming. Trusting in God, I find the future no longer scary.   AW

Week 27   Matthew 13:1-23
Changeable Soil (Sunday)

Sheri was looking over her mother's shoulder, watching her repot several plants on the kitchen table. "New soil means new growth," her mother chanted.

As Sheri walked out the back door, she thought of the parable of the sower, or the soils, as she had heard it called. She decided she had in her short, 17-year life, been repotted half a dozen times. She had been almost every kind of soil already.

She thought about the time she was on her way home from Sunday school. Third grade it was. She had learned some terrific truth and was running home to tell someone. Three junior-high boys started throwing mud chunks at her. She forgot her truth, she forgot her word, because of her trouble on the road.

She thought of a later time at ninth-grade Bible camp when everyone sang and prayed way past midnight. She had felt so close to God, so holy. The feelings lasted only a week or so after she got home. Was there no depth of soil? Why couldn't she hold on to those feelings?

These last couple of years it had been thorns. Her friends were thorns, and some of her school activities had been thorns—late games and band trips and a dozen other things that kept her from growing in God's Word.

Sheri walked through the backyard and out into the garden. She knelt down and picked up a handful of the cool spring soil. It formed itself into the palm of her hand and held its shape when she opened her palm. "I wish God would shape me like that. I wish he'd make me good soil, rich soil, deep soil, so his Word would grow in me."

As she knelt there in the garden, she prayed for that. It was a beginning.   SS

Smart? (Monday)

"The knowledge of the secrets of the kingdom of heaven has been given to you" (Matt. 13:11).

The secrets of science are pure mystery,
And modern computers drive me up a tree.
Approaching math'matics, frustration's the key.
I guess that I'm not very smart.

Shakespeare and Darwin are over my head.
I'll never remember what Kennedy said.
Who cares about Plato? My goodness, he's dead.
I guess that I'm not very smart.

I forget who it was who found Venus and Mars,
That Detroit is the city that makes lots of cars,
But I know who governs the moon and the stars.
I guess that I'm really quite smart.   KK

Grant to Me (Tuesday)

"Whoever has will be given more" (Matt. 13:12).

Lord,
you've given me so many things.
I don't deserve more from you.
But if it be your will,
grant that I may treat
   temper tantrums with self-control,
   false strength with gentleness,
   harsh manners with kindness,
   irritation with patience,
   dissension with peace,
   sadness with joy,
   and hatred with love,
because you do.   KK

Sensing (Wednesday)

"But blessed are your eyes because they see, and your ears because they hear" (Matt. 13:16).

I see
so much evil in the world, Lord.
Help me look past it
to the needs you see.

I hear
so many words that need not be said, Lord.
Help me listen through them
for the cries you hear.

I feel
so many hateful things, Lord.
Help me go beyond them
to give the love you give
to your children.   KK

Revelations (Thursday)

"But blessed are your eyes because they see, and your ears because they hear" (Matt. 13:16).

It's so easy to take things easy
when God seems a long way away.
God's not looking over your shoulder.
He doesn't have too much to say.

But God's there just the same and watching.
He knows how you're leading your life.
And it matters to him what you're doing.
Reality cuts like a knife.

God doesn't draw pictures or make a long speech.
He uses people to try to get through.
You ought to be watching and listening.
God's revealing great things to you.   KK

To Be or Not to Be (Friday)

"What was sown among the thorns is the man who hears the word, but the worries of this life and the deceitfulness of wealth choke it making it unfruitful" (Matt. 13:22).

Why be a Christian?
There's no 8½" by 11" membership certificate,
suitable for framing.
No autographed picture.
No official monthly magazine.
No discounts or giveaways.
No annual banquet.
No toll-free telephone number to answer your
questions.
No special previews of upcoming appearances.

Why be a Christian?
Because Jesus Lives.   KK

Thanks (Saturday)

"But what was sown on good soil is the man who hears the word and understands it. He produces a crop, yielding a hundred, sixty or thirty times what was sown" (Matt. 13:23).

Thank you, Lord, for changing me.
When I want to scream, I whisper a prayer,
and when I am lonely, I know you are there.
Going through times that would hurt or destroy,
in you I find strength and a new kind of joy.
You've made me look past my own little life
to things going on in a world full of strife.
When others walk paths I once traveled through,
I'm glad they can see the peace found in you.
Grant that I always may give you my love,
remembering everything comes from above.   KK

Week 28 Genesis 29
Equal Love (Sunday)

Was it only because Leah had weak eyes that Jacob chose Rachel? Probably not. Rachel was younger, perhaps more innocent. Maybe she was only 12 or 13 when Jacob first showed up. Seven years later when both she and her older sister were married, Rachel was maybe 19 or 20.

Whatever the reason—age, innocence, or weak eyes—Jacob loved Rachel more than Leah. Leah bore Jacob all those sons, but he still liked Rachel better. How did Leah handle that?

To be sure, marrying him wasn't her idea. Her father had tricked his nephew into that. But Leah didn't let on. When Jacob crawled into bed with her on their wedding night, she could have whispered, "I'm not Rachel; I'm Leah." She didn't. She continued her father's deception.

It's tough to live close together with someone who is more loved—or more favored. Leah found it hard not to be loved. Rachel found it hard to be barren and to watch her sister give birth to three healthy boys. Perhaps Jacob found it hard to have two bickering sisters on his hands.

Who in a family doesn't feel the inequity of love? What mom or dad or grandma or grandpa can be so careful in metering out love and affection and time and gifts so that each child feels fully and equally loved? For human parents such love is impossible.

It is not impossible for God. God so loved the world that he gave—and he gave Jesus to each of us and all of us fully and equally. We are completely loved by God. We need not compare ourselves with others, be jealous of others, or even notice how others seem to be loved. We are loved as well, as fully, and as deeply as anyone.   SS

Thanks for Relatives (Monday)

"You are my own flesh and blood" (Gen. 29:14).

I was eager to get to Sioux City to visit our relatives. We hadn't been there for a long time.

My uncles and aunts and cousins have a very special place in my affection. Perhaps that's because I come from a small family, and our relatives live far away. But I believe many larger families feel the same way about their kinsfolk.

When relatives live too much of their lives together, they can quarrel like anyone else. But try insulting someone's relatives, and you will quickly find that blood is indeed thicker than water.

I thank God for my relatives, the larger family that God has given me. I try to remember them often in my prayers.   JJS

It's Only Skin Deep (Tuesday)

"Rachel was lovely in form and beautiful" (Gen. 29:17).

I'm often amazed at the way boys choose their dates. It's only natural that physical beauty should play a part in such a selection. However, there is another kind of beauty that boys often seem to overlook.

Many girls who do not have great outward beauty do have the beauty of joyful dispositions, pleasing personalities, or loving and tender hearts.

There is a third kind of beauty even more overlooked. God gives some a beauty at birth which in time whithers away like a flower. But God also gives many a beauty when through his Son they are reborn into his kingdom and live as his loving, obedient children. That kind of spiritual beauty does not fade but blooms forever.   JJS

How Time Flies (Wednesday)

"So Jacob served seven years to get Rachel, but they seemed like only a few days to him because of his love for her" (Gen. 29:20).

There are a few couples in my congregation who have been married more than 60 years. That seems like a very long time to be married, especially when you consider the short duration of some marriages today. But to the couples it hasn't seemed long at all.

What can make seven years seem but a few days, or 60 years seem but a few years? Only the power of true love and devotion.

Jacob's self-sacrificing love for Rachel reminds us of the still deeper love of Christ for his church. How good to know that someone loves us that much!   JJS

Dirty Tricks (Thursday)

"When morning came, there was Leah!" (Gen. 29:25).

The break-in and cover-up that we know as the Watergate affair did much to undermine the confidence of the American public in our politicians. It has taken many years and a lot of effort on the part of honest politicians to regain the respect that was lost by the foolish deeds of a few.

Jacob who tricked his father and angered his brother did not gain much but years of hard work in a foreign country. Likewise, Laban, his father-in-law, who tricked Jacob into marrying Leah, later lost the love and respect of both his daughters through his dirty tricks.

The Lord has called us to be honest in our dealings with others. Honesty is still the best policy.   JJS

Teacher's Pet (Friday)

"He loved Rachel more than Leah" (Gen. 29:30)

Have you ever known a teacher who played favorites with students? I have seen a lot of students with hurt feelings as a result.

The teacher's pet gets attention while the rest of the students' questions go unanswered. The teacher's pet gets chosen to sing the solo or recite the reading while others more qualified are left out. The teacher's pet plays the whole game while others play only a few minutes.

Jacob loved Rachel more than Leah. But Jacob also apparently showed favoritism for her children over those of Leah. His partiality for Joseph caused a lot of family grief later on.

I am glad that our Lord shows no partiality.   JJS

Overcoming Handicaps (Saturday)

"She named him Judah" (Gen. 29:35).

Handicaps come in many forms. People who have disabilities are handicapped by buildings designed only for so-called normal people. But people are also handicapped by prejudices and favoritism.

Many handicaps can be overcome. Ludwig van Beethoven, for instance, composed some wonderful music after he became deaf.

Leah's handicap was that Jacob loved Rachel more than Leah. Yet God helped Leah overcome this handicap as she gave birth to six sons and a daughter, children who were very important to Jacob. Furthermore, it was Judah, Leah's son, who was the ancestor of David and Jesus.

If we only ask, the Lord will help each of us live to the best of our ability and to God's glory.   JJS

Week 29   Luke 19:1-10
Short Stuff (Sunday)

Maybe that's why he became a tax collector.
Zacchaeus, that is. Because he was short. "I'll show
them," he may have said when he was a kid. "I'll show
them all." And he did. He became rich. Zacchaeus had
people's grudging respect. If a tax collector like
Zacchaeus decided that you had to pay such and so many
silver or gold pieces, or so many bushels of grain, that's
what you paid. There were no tax schedules, no
standards. The tax collector eyeballed each person and
decided how much he would—or could—pay. He could
be bribed into changing that, though.

I suppose the rich and the crooked had the tax system
as well beat in those days as they do today.

Is it any wonder that tax collectors were hated? Is it
any wonder they were called "sinners" along with
prostitutes, criminals, and other riffraff? Is it any wonder
that Jesus was criticized by the religious community for
going home for supper with Zacchaeus?

Zacchaeus showed them. He was one of the short
people, but by collaboration with the Romans and by
knowing the economic nerve-fibers of the community,
and by keeping the very wealthy in his pocket, he had
risen above his stature and his reputation. You can be
sure no one called him "Shorty" anymore—at least no
one who paid taxes in his district.

But if Zacchaeus did his tax business in a big way, he
did his conversion in a big way too. He came down from
the tree, went home for supper, then rose to high heaven
on the wings of Jesus' teaching.

"I'll give away half of what I own to the poor," he
shouted. "And if I've cheated anyone, I'll pay it back
four times over." That's a pretty good start toward a new
life. Zacchaeus—a big man.   SS

Follow Me (Monday)

"He wanted to see who Jesus was, but being a short man he could not, because of the crowd" (Luke 19:3).

"Zac, follow your conscience instead of the crowd. You weren't getting any closer to me by following the crowd," said Jesus.

"Yeah, the crowd wouldn't let me get near you. Kept telling me, 'You're a sinner. Jesus isn't going to have anything to do with you.' "

"Two thousand years from now, Zac," Jesus said, "crowds will still turn people away from me. 'Hey, come have fun with us. You don't need that Jesus stuff. Sin is human nature—enjoy yourself. Follow us,' crowds will say. 'Follow me,' I say. What do you say?" KL

Forgive Yourself (Tuesday)

"So he ran ahead and climbed a sycamore-fig tree to see him" (Luke 19:4).

"Jesus, how could I possibly follow you? If I decided to lead a Christian life, I would surely fail to measure up."

"Zac, I have already forgiven your shortcomings. And because I forgive you, you can forgive yourself. Come down from the high tree of alienation from God and other people. God's pardon wipes out the past. The marks of the past may remain, but they become a reminder of redeeming grace. I can raise you to great heights by giving you a new life in me." KL

I Choose You (Wednesday)

"He has gone to be a guest of a 'sinner' " (Luke 19:7).

"I want to stay at your house while I'm in town," Jesus said to an astonished Zacchaeus.

"Sir, I sin. I cheat. I lie. I'm no good."

"Look Zac, it wouldn't matter if you lived in the 20th century and got buzzed on Miller and fooled around with your girl in the backseat of your Chevy every chance you had."

"Pardon me, sir?"

"The point is, I choose you—sin or no sin."

"And I have no say in the matter?"

"Oh, sure, you can walk away from me anytime, but I won't let you go without a fight."

"You're going to hit me?"

"Yep, in the conscience, where it counts."   KL

Jesus Is Faithful (Thursday)

"So [Zacchaeus] came down at once and welcomed him gladly" (Luke 19:5-6).

"Jesus, when you said you'd raise me up to new heights, I thought I'd feel taller. Now that I'm a Christian, why don't I feel changed?"

"Zac, when we first met, you followed me with the eagerness of your newly discovered faith in me. We both felt joyous."

"But, Lord, since I don't feel that way every day, there must be something wrong with my faith!"

"No, Zac, it's not your faith that sustains our relationship. I know what it is to be human. It is my willingness to forgive and my faithfulness that sustains and brings Christian joy."   KL

The Joy of Eternity (Friday)

"Today salvation has come to this house" (Luke 19:9).

"Jesus, leading a Christian life requires so many sacrifices—saying no when I want to say yes, caring when I don't have time, sharing when I need it all. Isn't life supposed to be fun?"

"Zac, I want your life to be fun, but I also want you to experience the joy of eternity. Your time on earth is microseconds compared to your time in eternity with me. You are only on the first step of your walk with me. Like a toddler learning to walk, you will fall many times. Remember that if you will let me help you up again and give you courage, you will experience not just fun, but eternal joy."   KL

To Save the Lost (Saturday)

"The Son of Man came to seek and to save the lost" (Luke 19:10).

"Zac, practicing your faith includes upholding your morals. Satan will tempt you to let your morals fall. Don't play with those temptations, saying 'I'll think about it,' or 'I'll just try it once,' hoping Satan won't continue to chase you. He will. He'll chase you with these temptations until you have no idea where you stand on any issues. You'll be lost.

"But I will find you and bring you back to me. I will love you no matter how far you have strayed and no matter whom you have become. For I have come to save the lost."   KL

Week 30 Psalm 8
A Little Less than God (Sunday)

When we read the headlines in the morning paper—murder, hit-and-run, rape, graft, corruption—we wouldn't think humans were created only just a little less than God or the heavenly beings. But Psalm 8 says so. We humans have been given all of God's creation as our home, our playground, and our management area.

Psalm 8 is echoed in some memorable lines from *Hamlet*. Now you may or may not have fallen in love with Shakespeare in your high-school English class, but you have to admit these are impressive lines:

> What a piece of work is man! how noble in reason!
> how infinite in faculty! in form and moving how
> express and admirable! in action how like an
> angel! in apprehension how like a god!

Many of our forefathers and mothers took all of these marvelous descriptions too seriously and set out on a course of roughshod domination of the world.

By the year 2000 this continent will have been "civilized" for 500 years. In that time we have polluted the Great Lakes, acid-rained the Northeast, the Upper Midwest, and much of Canada, dust-bowled the Southwest twice, dried up three mighty rivers, and put a fair amount of our precious topsoil down other rivers, or off to the four winds. We have buried our poisons—only to have them reemerge in our drinking water.

Humankind is indeed a marvelous piece of work, but we soon must apply our marvelous minds to loving our world and caring for it and restoring it—no matter what it costs. Where the people rule, no person, principality, parliament, or power should be allowed to ravage the air, the land, or the water. These are God's gifts, God's heritage to us all. SS

God Is Great (Monday)

"How majestic is your name in all the earth!" (Ps. 8:1).

I've always wondered what it would be like to have written one of the many books in the Bible. I think I'd keep it simple and blunt, similar to the way so many other people did in the Bible. For example, "I praise you because your works are wonderful" (Ps. 139:14).

All this may seem a little silly, but it's true. Our God is the only God and is greater than anyone or anything in the entire universe. Our God is the creator of ourselves and everything around us.

Let's see here. Jay 1:1, "God is great, and out of everyone's league." Hmm—I like that.   JAB

God's Defense (Tuesday)

"From the lips of children and infants you have ordained praise because of your enemies, to silence the foe and the avenger" (Ps. 8:2).

There are many types of defenses. There is a defense in football, a national defense, and even such a thing as defensive driving. But all defenses have at least one thing in common. They protect one's self, team, or country from someone else attacking.

God provides a defense for us as well, defense against our worst enemy—Satan. As Christians we are Satan's prime target, but under God's defense we are protected from the harms of the devil and all his empty promises.

JAB

Why Do You Love Me? *(Wednesday)*

"What is man that you are mindful of him?" (Ps. 8:4).

You know, Lord, things haven't been goin' so great recently. I guess I haven't been living a good Christian life lately either. But what do you expect? You know I flunked my third algebra test today? I hate Mr. Evans! I bet if you put a red cape on him he'd turn into Supermath. Craig hasn't helped my problems either. I know I shouldn't have beat him up, but did you hear the names he called me? Besides he threw the first punch. Yes, I know, turn the other cheek, right?

Lord, why do you put up with me? I'm a real jerk, yet you love me anyway. I suppose that shows me how blessed I really am. Thanks, Lord.   JAB

God's Little Kids *(Thursday)*

"What is. . . the son of man that you care for him?" (Ps. 8:4).

Everyone is born completely helpless. For an infant to survive, it needs constant care for many years. Children must be fed, bathed, and have their diapers changed every day. This love and care comes from the parents or other loved ones.

Birth is one of God's most remarkable forms of creation. We are children of God, as well as children of our human parents. God is our heavenly Father. We are God's children, and he loves and cares for us all.   JAB

The Best for Last (Friday)

"You have made him a little lower than the heavenly beings" (Ps. 8:5).

In the beginning God made light.
From that he made day, and then he made night.
Next he made water the same time as heaven.
The third day God called forth some good dry land,
so bushes and trees and other plants could stand.
The sun and moon arrived on the fourth day.
The birds and fish showed up on the fifth.
The rest of the animals came on the sixth.
Then God made us just less than himself,
And has us care for everything else.   JAB

Babysitters for God's World (Saturday)

"You made him ruler over the works of your hands" (Ps. 8:6).

I have found through personal experience that babysitting isn't always an easy job. It's a job that takes a great deal of love and responsibility. Sitters have the trust of every parent to care for the child as if the child were their own.

God gave us the responsibility to care for the land, sea, and everything else he created. This also is a job that takes a lot of love and responsibility, but God trusts us to care for all his creations. With the trust God has in us, shouldn't we show responsibility to care?   JAB

Week 31   Acts 9:1-31

Zapped by God (Sunday)

Don't we wish, sometimes, that God would zap us as he did St. Paul. Paul was marching headlong down his wrongheaded path when God zapped him. One moment he was "breathing out murderous threats against the Lord's disciples," and the next minute he was lightning-bolted to the ground—blinded and shouting wild responses to a voice from the sky.

This wasn't a vision out of Paul's wild imagination. Even those on the road with Paul heard the voice. This was an honest-to-goodness, right-out-of-heaven, zap from God.

No wonder Paul was so dedicated and positive about everything he did after that. No wonder he made such a terrific missionary. No wonder he was willing to endure so much—the ridicule, the beatings, the shipwrecks, the imprisonments.

No wonder. All Paul had to do was shut his eyes and remember his former blindness. All he had to do was spend a few silent moments by himself, and that booming voice from heaven would come back. Don't we wish, sometimes, that God would zap us as he did St. Paul?

Chances are God won't. Chances are the nearest thing to a zapping you and I will get will be a few tears during a sermon, a bit of choking up during a funeral, a kind of warm feeling now and then as we pray.

How can we know then? How can we be sure—as St. Paul was sure? Maybe none of us will ever be quite that sure, but we can believe and know without being zapped. Remember Jesus' words to Thomas? "Because you have seen me, you have believed; blessed are those who have not seen and yet have believed."

That's us—never zapped, and yet we believe. Blessed. Wow!   SS

Don't Be Left in the Dark   (Monday)

"As he neared Damascus on his journey, suddenly a light from heaven flashed around him" (Acts 9:3).

The glory of God comes to us in many different forms. We remember Jesus Christ in many different forms. We remember Jesus Christ in the Lord's Supper. In Baptism, water helps us see God's love. In the Bible, one of the most common vehicles of God is light.

Saul was struck down by light. That light was Jesus Christ showing himself to Saul, whose life was changed from then on.

Spiritual light is a gift from God that enables us to see everything in a new way. If God wasn't with us, lighting our way, we would be lost in darkness.   AW

Report for Duty (Tuesday)

"Now get up and go into the city, and you will be told what you must do" (Acts 9:6).

Wouldn't it be great if we could report for duty somewhere and have God tell us exactly what to do?

It's not that easy. Reporting for duty is important, but the steps that follow are not always clear. Sometimes we feel as if we are stuck in neutral. We wonder what God wants us to do with our life and what talents we have, if any, that God could use.

God made each of us different, and that in itself is a special gift. God wants us to explore our own individuality and out of that to discover our talents and put our faith in action. God's loving acceptance will stand behind us.   AW

A Follower of God (Wednesday)

"But the Lord said to Ananias, 'Go! This man is my chosen instrument to carry my name before the Gentiles and their kings and before the children of Israel' " (Acts 9:15).

Paul was one of the greatest Christian leaders in the New Testament. It seems curious, though, why God chose Paul to be an apostle. Paul, who was called Saul before his conversion, had arrested and persecuted many Christians. Still, God picked Paul to do great things for God's kingdom.

God has chosen us, too, to be his followers and to share his love. It doesn't make sense that God would pick *us*, either. Yet, we can be glad that we, like Paul, have been chosen to be followers of God.   AW

New Directions   (Thursday)

"Brother Saul, the Lord. . . has sent me so that you may see again and be filled with the Holy Spirit" (Acts 9:17).

God wants to give new vision and direction to what we surrender to him. Paul's former religious training served him well as a Christian apostle because God helped him see his learning in a new light.

What does it mean to set aside our former ways and let God run the show? Does it mean giving up our present interests and talents in music, acting, or sports? It could be, but God may also want to empower us to see and use those gifts in new ways.   AW

Can I Be a Christian? (Friday)

"Immediately, something like scales fell from Saul's eyes, and he could see again. He got up and was baptized" (Acts 9:18).

Can I be a Christian? God wants us all to be Christians and gladly welcomes us into his family through Baptism. Yet even though we've been baptized, we sometimes wonder whether we are Christians, because of the bad things we have done.

God knows everything about us, even the bad things. And still, God seeks to forgive us. In spite of the terrible way Saul had persecuted Christians, God still sought him out and made him his own. God wants you and me, too, to know that whatever we have done, we belong to him. We are Christians. AW

Encouragement (Saturday)

"Yet Saul grew more and more powerful and baffled the Jews living in Damascus by proving that Jesus is the Christ" (Acts 9:22).

Encouragement is a great way to give someone confidence and inspiration. Recently my sister handed me a poem she had written to encourage me. It really gave me a lift. What would we do without friends and loved ones?

When they are not at hand, the Bible is one place to turn. When I read about Saul's conversion and learned how God took a man who worked against his kingdom and turned his life around, I was encouraged. It helped me believe that God wants to use me too. Through other people and through the Bible, God encourages and strengthens *our* witness. AW

Week 32   1 Samuel 17:55—18:5; 19:1-7; 20:30-42

Instant Friendship (Sunday)

David and Jonathan were friends at first sight. King Saul took David into his own home and kept him there because of his son Jonathan's friendship. David spent some years in Saul's household. There he learned how a king lives and how a king acts and how a king rules. These would be valuable lessons in years to come.

David learned some things about King Saul as well. Saul had fits of depression or paranoia. When one of Saul's fits was upon him, he became jealous of David and tried to kill him. David dodged several spears and twice ran away to preserve his life.

Through all this Jonathan remained David's faithful friend. Jonathan repeatedly warned him, brought him reports when he was in hiding, and in one case even talked his father Saul into taking David back.

A friend like that is worth a lot. When we're young, we sometimes choose friends more for quantity than quality. Having dozens and scores of casual friends but no really close one doesn't help much. The book of Proverbs got it just right 3000 years ago:

A man of many companions may come to ruin,
but there is a friend who sticks closer than
a brother [or sister].

There is something special about that very close friend, that someone you can trust with every secret, with every hope and fear, someone you would trust with your very life. Jesus is such a friend—as we sing in the hymn, "What a privilege to carry *everything* to him in prayer." David and Jonathan were such friends. You may have another such friend already. If you're really blessed, you will marry such a friend.   SS

Taking Off the Armor (Monday)

"And Jonathan made a covenant with David" (1 Sam. 18:3).

A best friend is someone to share your innermost thoughts with and know that they're safe. There is no need for "armor" or pretenses between friends.

Perhaps David and Jonathan became friends for that reason. David was a young boy fighting in Saul's army, far from home. Jonathan, the king's son, held a position of power so he couldn't make friends easily. They both must have felt very alone in their different ways, and they needed each other. Because of that need, there was no reason for any pretense between them—they didn't have to try to impress one another. When Jonathan gave his robe to David, it showed that each could be himself in the presence of the other.   EMB

Trusting Friends (Tuesday)

"Jonathan was very fond of David" (1 Sam. 19:1).

Every friendship needs trust to survive. A friendship is born when two people begin to trust each other, a friendship grows as trust in one another grows, and friendship can be destroyed by the destruction of trust in a relationship. You can trust a friend with a secret, a possession, a fault.

David trusted Jonathan with his life. Even though Jonathan was the king's son, David trusted his friend to go against the king's orders to kill him. David's trust was well-placed; the power of their love and friendship was stronger than Saul's hatred of David.

Today, most of us aren't forced to test our trust in one another as drastically as David had to, but trust is just as important in a friendship now as it was then.   EMB

I'm Counting on You (Wednesday)

"Saul listened to Jonathan" (1 Sam. 19:6).

A friend is there when you need someone the most. You can always count on a friend to share both the good and the bad. A good example is David and Jonathan. Jonathan was David's only hope, the only one who could save David's life. Jonathan pleaded David's case before his father the king, and was able to keep Saul from killing his friend. He did this out of friendship, a very special kind of love.

Love is one of our most basic needs, and friendship is a fundamental way of fulfilling that need. Jonathan's love for David, stronger than his obedience to his father, gave him the courage to save an innocent man's life. A special friendship can often give us the courage to stand up for something we feel is right.   EMB

Two Together (Thursday)

"Jonathan became one in spirit with David" (1 Sam. 18:1).

David,
a poor man of no repute.
Jonathan,
a king's son.
An unlikely twosome for a closeness
greater than that of brothers.
A bond thicker than blood
would save a man's life.
All because of a friendship
that the shepherd in the field
and the cultured prince would say
could never happen.
Maybe a God-given friend isn't so bad.
Where will your next friend come from?   EMB

Friendships Old and New (Friday)

"Jonathan. . . came to love [David] as much as he loved himself" (1. Sam. 18:1 TEV).

It's not easy to say good-bye to good friends, and the prospect of making new friends can be frightening. When many of my friends graduated from high school, I was left with two more years. At first I was lonely. I missed my older friends and feared losing contact with them. But I still had friends in my own class, and I started to realize that there were a lot of neat people in my class whom I'd never noticed before.

It was lucky for David that Jonathan wasn't too preoccupied with himself to realize that David could be a new friend. Sometimes we can miss out on worthwhile friendships because we're too preoccupied with ourselves and other things. Even focusing on old friendships can keep us from making new ones.   EMB

Separation (Saturday)

"Then Jonathan said to David, 'Go in peace' " (1 Sam. 20:42).

After high school, many friends will go separate ways. But can the miles between friends separate a friendship? No, when two people can share one another's pains, joys, and company, they can't really be separated by mere miles. Deep inside, there are memories of the good times, and a glow when one realizes that somewhere there is a friend who can be counted on to care.

When Saul threatened David's life, David and Jonathan were faced with the possibility that they might not see each other again. Yet, by just knowing one another and crossing paths, they held something very dear in their hearts, and their lives were richer for the experience. Our lives, too, are enriched by friends, however far away.   EMB

Week 33   Luke 7:36-50
Big Trouble (Sunday)

Art had been in almost every kind of trouble a middle-years teenager could get into. He had shoplifted, stolen a car, used and sold drugs, gotten a girl pregnant, and more. Then he got religion. Strange thing, the judge believed it. Pastor Williams showed up at the trial and spoke on Art's behalf. That helped convince the judge.

Art stood up to face his sentence. He was sentenced to many hours of volunteer work with United Fund agencies and at the retirement center, too, but his jail sentence was suspended. He was paroled to Pastor Williams.

If anyone could have seen Art's eyes at that moment, and a few minutes later when Pastor Williams went over and gave him a gigantic hug, there would have been very few doubts. Art loved Pastor Williams and was thankful for his second chance.

Back at church, though, it wasn't so easy. Stan, the youth group president, was the toughest. He didn't really oppose Art or make it outwardly hard for him, but there was a quiet resentment. Pastor Williams knew he had a problem—and he knew the problem at this stage was more with Stan than with Art.

At a youth meeting the pastor talked about God's will. He said that things like stealing and misusing sex were sins, and that those who did things like that needed to repent. But he also said that God forgives *all* the sins of *everyone* who trusts in Jesus.

Then the pastor said that some of the worst sins of all aren't usually reported in the newspaper. People can be destroyed by things like jealousy, anger, and an unforgiving spirit. Attitudes like that are condemned by the Bible, and they can tear a congregation or a youth group apart. He looked at Stan when he was saying this.

Later that evening, Stan whispered to the pastor, "Thanks." It was a start.   SS

In the Pharisee's House (Monday)

"Now one of the Pharisees invited Jesus to have dinner with him, so he went into the Pharisee's house" (Luke 7:36).

Over the years the Pharisees have acquired a bad reputation. We picture them as conceited hypocrites who think they deserve God's special favor. In the Gospels they have frequent run-ins with Jesus.

This simple text shows us, however, that Jesus came to save all people. He associated with both the "sinners" and the Pharisees. He ate with both. God wants all people to be in his kingdom, and he invites all to his table. His love is for all: poor and rich, weak and strong, young and old, timid and brave. He invites us to set aside our own ideas of worth and rely on his grace alone.

PJR

Touched by a Sinner! (Tuesday)

"If this man were a prophet, he would know who is touching him and what kind of woman she is—that she is a sinner" (Luke 7:39).

Of course Jesus knew! As God's Son, he had come to seek and to save the lost. He knew she was a sinner. And he forgave her. Simon, Jesus' host that day, couldn't believe that Jesus would let this "woman of the city" touch him, let alone forgive her. But forgive her he did! Jesus' love for all people is so great that all can be forgiven.

So we should not put others down and label them "sinners" because we think we are better than they are. Instead, why not introduce them to the Savior that they too might receive his forgiving love? PJR

A Certain Creditor (Wednesday)

"Two men owed money to a certain moneylender" (Luke 7:41).

Jesus often used parables to make his point. A parable makes one stop and think and then make a decision.

Simon, the Pharisee who had invited Jesus in for a meal, was horrified that Jesus let a woman who was a sinner bathe his feet and anoint him.

Jesus' response was this parable: A kindly creditor forgave the debts of both people who owed him money. It would be natural for the one who had been forgiven the most to love the creditor the most. "Therefore, Simon, why are you so surprised that this woman shows me so much love?" is what Jesus means. "Why not show more love yourself, and why not rejoice with her? Don't I love you too?"   PJR

Which Are Many (Thursday)

"Her many sins have been forgiven" (Luke 7:47).

A young man lived a life of crime to support his drug addiction. After several years he was arrested, convicted, and sent to prison. In prison he met a chaplain who listened to him and talked with him about God's love for sinners. He told him how Christ died and rose again for all people, even him. The young man repented of his many sins, and confessed his faith.

You never saw a happier person! He was so relieved to be rid of his burden of guilt. He reestablished contact with his family, and he volunteered to tutor other prisoners. His love for others showed that he had been forgiven much!   PJR

Who Is This? (Friday)

"Who is this who even forgives sins?" (Luke 7:49).

It was enough to make anyone wonder. First an uninvited woman wandered into the house seeking Jesus. Then she washed his feet with her tears and anointed him with precious ointment. Next Jesus asked the host why he hadn't done the same thing. But the last straw was Jesus praising the sinful woman's actions and telling her that her sins were forgiven. Who would dare to forgive sins?

How thankful we are that we know who this is! It is Jesus the Christ, sent by the Father to be the world's Savior. Who is this? It is the Lamb who was slain, whose blood set us free to be people of God. It is our privilege to tell others who this is! PJR

Go in Peace (Saturday)

"Jesus said to the woman, 'Your faith has saved you; go in peace' " (Luke 7:50).

This woman, who had been an outcast, experienced a major turnabout in her life. In coming to Jesus she had admitted her sinfulness, and she had heard him say to her, "Your sins are forgiven." She was now a new person. She had a future. Then Jesus said to her, "Go in peace."

In some churches those same words are used at the end of each Holy Communion service. The worship leader says, "Go in peace. Serve the Lord," and we respond, "Thanks be to God." Just as this woman was made whole by Jesus, so are we restored by his forgiving love. We too can "go in peace." We are made well to serve. PJR

Week 34   Psalm 34
Fears (Sunday)

"I sought the Lord, and he answered me; he delivered me from all my fears." Linda had done this a dozen times. She had come back to this psalm and this verse dozens of times in her evening devotions.

"Why am I so afraid of everything?" she asked. "Why can't I take God at his word?" She scanned the Bible verses that came to mind: "walking through the valley of the shadow"—"fear no evil"—and one from somewhere in Paul's letters, "have no anxiety about anything."

"I have anxiety about *everything*," she said to herself. Linda's Sunday school teacher was about the most sensible woman she knew. She decided to talk to her after Sunday school:

"Mrs. Gardner, could I talk to you?"

"Sure Linda, what about?"

"My fears."

"Fears?"

"I'm afraid of almost everything."

"You too?" Mrs. Gardner said, smiling.

They talked right through the second church service. Linda decided that if even a person like Mrs. Gardner, who seemed to have it all together, if even *she* had fears, then maybe fear wasn't all that bad.

They talked about foolish fears, and the fears of looking foolish.

"Knowing God loves me, knowing I am a child of God, that gave me confidence at last," Mrs. Gardner said. "I can stand up in church and read. I can play a solo in the summer band. I can make a speech at my women's group. Could you do that?"

"Never," Linda said, smiling.

"You will. You'll learn to think less about yourself and more about what God wants to do through you."   SS

It's Not Always That Easy (Monday)

"I will extol the Lord at all times" (Ps. 34:1).

My dog just died, and I am supposed to have faith. I just missed being on the state basketball team, and I'm told to pray for other people who made the team. It's not always that easy!

David wrote that we should bless the Lord at all times—not just when we are in a good mood but also when we are upset. Then, too, we should believe that God is at work. Maybe it can best be summarized by saying, "The Lord works in mysterious ways."

I'm sure glad God has a lot of patience, because with me he'll need a lot. Maybe someday I won't doubt, and I really will be able to bless the Lord at all times. Maybe.

TLM

God Works through Us (Tuesday)

"His praise will always be on my lips" (Ps. 34:1).

Recently a friend of mine broke up with her boyfriend. They had been very close, and she took the break-up extremely hard.

When she called me to tell me of the break-up she only fell deeper into her depression. She started to tell me how her life meant nothing anymore and that she didn't want to go on.

I became worried. I was afraid that she might try to kill herself. It was in that moment of desperation that I found myself turning to God.

In the end, my friend was helped to get over her loss. Although she hasn't admitted it, I know that it was with God's help that she made it through.

TLM

Praise God Together (Wednesday)

"Let us exalt his name together" (Ps. 34:3).

At church, on retreats, or with other families, it is more enjoyable to praise God together.

At Christian youth retreats, I feel so close to everyone. It seems that every time I go to a gathering where Christians are, I make instant friendships. People that I just met end up closer than brothers and sisters to me.

By exalting the Lord's name together we become closer not only to God but to each other.

Let us exalt his name together.   TLM

Through All the Pain (Thursday)

"I sought the Lord, and he answered me" (Ps. 34:4).

A friend of mine and her sister were recently in a car accident. Her sister died in that accident. The driver of the car was drunk, but they rode with him anyway. My friend felt tremendously guilty. She thought that if she had spoken up she could have saved her sister's life.

She was depressed for weeks, and no one could reach her—no one except God. Even though she didn't know it, my friend needed God, and he was there for her, helping her through all the pain.

Just as God was there for her, he is there for us every time we are in pain, helping us to cope with it.   TLM

Liver! Uck! (Friday)

"O taste and see that the Lord is good" (Ps. 34:8).

"Mom, I can't eat that. It looks gross!"

We've all heard or spoken those words at least a hundred times. We are all afraid to try new things. Why eat liver? Nobody else likes it!

We can say the same thing about our faith. Why try God? None of my friends have!

The psalmist wrote the above verse in the hope that we would "taste" the faith.

Now that you have "tasted" and realized that there is something special about your faith in God, help somebody else. Help a friend or a stranger to "taste and see that the Lord is good."   TLM

Forty-Six Yards to Go (Saturday)

"The Lord. . .saves those who are crushed in spirit" (Ps. 34:18).

Forty-six yards to go and only seconds left. The team needed a miracle to win. Somehow they got that miracle and won the championship.

On that day the spirits of Jeff, the team's star running back, were flying. The future looked bright. Before long, he was signed by an NFL team. Then came the day he dived into a shallow lake and became paralyzed from the waist down.

Jeff isolated himself from his friends, his family, and his church. But they didn't forget him.

We all have times when we feel alone and isolated. We may even doubt our faith, but God is always with us. It's often when we are crushed in spirit that the Lord is present and ministering to us.   TLM

Week 35   Mark 9:33-50
The Millstone Necktie (Sunday)

How seldom we see ourselves as examples to others. We ourselves look up to certain people—our parents, friends, certain teachers, coaches. We pattern bits and pieces of our lives by what we see in others.

What we can't always recognize is that some people younger than ourselves look up to *us*. They watch us carefully, patterning their lives after ours, planning and dreaming ahead to a time when they can be like us.

Younger brothers and sisters are particularly apt to do this. They love us, they watch us, they want to be like us. If we drive carefully (or carelessly), they watch us. If we gossip or laugh at our friends behind their backs, they emulate us. If we care for ourselves—our health and well-being—they imitate us. If we are self-starters when it comes to church and Sunday school, they are apt to be that way too.

Jesus dealt us a pretty stern warning on this one. He had a child, maybe children, on his lap there in Capernaum. It may have been Peter's house, possibly Peter's children. Jesus warned us all: cause a child to sin and you'd be better off if a millstone were tied around your neck and you were pitched into the sea. Jesus, obviously, doesn't take kindly to our setting poor examples or causing children to go bad.

So we have a job to do, most of us, on our public image. It matters what we say, how we act, even how we look. Our example is everywhere apparent to the little ones around us. We are to befriend them, protect them, set them good examples. Jesus said, "Whoever welcomes one of these little children in my name welcomes me."

SS

The Servant of All (Monday)

"If anyone wants to be first, he must be the very last, and the servant of all" (Mark 9:35).

Everyone in his congregation thought he would retire, but he didn't. Instead, this man joined the Red Cross and spent most of his time going around the world, sharing the pain of many unfortunate people.

He was neither rich nor famous. Yet he discovered more happiness in helping people than in advancing his own career. With the assistance of the Red Cross, he went to countries where people were tortured by disease and illness. Sometimes he even went to war zones to take care of wounded soldiers and to bury their dead. To many people his work was not important, yet he was truly a servant of all. THP

Christian Language (Tuesday)

"Anyone who gives you a cup of water in my name because you belong to Christ will certainly not lose his reward" (Mark 9:41).

After a violent storm, our boat was losing its direction. The engine was badly damaged and didn't work. The boat drifted on the sea for a few days until finally a strange boat approached us. It was a fishing boat, but the fishermen did not speak our language.

While we tried to communicate, one of them noticed the cross I wore around my neck. He said something to the others, and they all smiled at me. Through their gesture, I understood that they were Christians, too. They were able to repair our engine, and they supplied us with food and water. Before they left, I gave them my cross. THP

Hands (Wednesday)

"If your hand causes you to sin, cut it off" (Mark 9:43).

I have always liked to draw. Though not good enough to be an artist, I still received many compliments from my friends in school. "You are very skillful with your hands," one said. When I heard that, I was thankful to God who gave me talented hands.

Yet, while my hands bring me pride, joy, and praise, they also lead to shame, sorrow, and criticism. I feel bad whenever I use my hands to do a sinful act against the Lord. God is hurt when I cannot keep my hands from doing wrong.

I need to remember who gave me these hands. When I am tempted to use them in evil ways, I need to remind myself to rely on God and ask for his guidance.   THP

Struggle (Thursday)

"And if your eye causes you to sin, pluck it out" (Mark 9:47).

A stack of homework lay on the table, untouched. Nearby, Leon sat on the chair, his head nodding sleepily. He wanted to open his eyes to pray before going to bed, but he couldn't. Inside a struggle was going on.

"Leave him alone. He's tired," Mind spoke.

"No, he needs to pray right now, and you better stop tempting him," came the voice of Faith.

"Me? Tempting him? I'm just helping him save his energy for tomorrow. Why does he need to pray anyway?"

"Because he loves God."

Leon suddenly awoke. In the silence of the night there was only God, who would hear his prayers.   THP

Temptation (Friday)

"It is better for you to enter the Kingdom of God with one eye then to have two eyes and be thrown into hell" (Mark 9:47).

Dennis thought they were his friends, or at least they had been. They now turned their backs on him just because he refused to take their drugs. He also felt very irritated when they called him "coward," "sissy" or "chicken."

Several times Dennis was tempted to take drugs to prove he was a part of the group. But inside him there was a voice warning, "That's wrong, Dennis. Taking drugs is not only a crime against society but also a serious sin against God, since you are destroying your own healthy body."

"Try this. It gives you guts," they again insisted.

Dennis shook his head. As he walked away, he mumbled to himself, "I would rather lose all of you than lose God by committing a stupid sin against him."   THP

Salt (Saturday)

"Salt is good, but if it loses its saltiness, how can you make it salty again?" (Mark 9:50).

My chemistry teacher calls it sodium chloride. To me, though, salt is a natural substance I use on my meals every day. As far as I know, salt is used in three ways: seasoning food, preserving food, and cleansing. It helps to enhance a meal's flavor, to keep food unspoiled for a long period of time, and sometimes to wash off dirty spots on clothes or to prevent the infection of a wound.

Being a Christian, I'm also "salt of the earth." My faith is the saltiness. I need the saltiness—faith—to spread the Christian flavor to others. I need it to preserve myself from sin, and finally, to cleanse away the sins I have committed.   THP

Week 36   Genesis 4:1-16

A Favorable Offering (Sunday)

It sounds like prejudice, doesn't it, this story of Cain and Abel? It sounds as if God, for no reason, chose Abel's offering, actually favored it, over Cain's. "The Lord looked with favor on Abel and his offering, but on Cain and his offering he did not look with favor."

If God can be prejudiced against us, what hope is there? I mean, if before I ever get a chance, God rejects me, things are going to be pretty tough.

Actually, the implications of the story are probably that God reads hearts—and Cain's heart wasn't in his offering. He was jealous of his brother, he hated him, and in time he killed him. If God looks at the heart, there *is* some hope.

We have yet another reason for hope—the person and teachings of Jesus Christ, our Savior. For instance, take Jesus' story of the Pharisee and the tax collector. Again God looked at the heart. Again God judged motivation and attitude as the offering was being made. God plays no favorites.

It's scary, knowing that God can see into our innermost motivations. It's scary that God knows why I do everything—that I go to youth group mainly because Sandy goes and I want to be near her—or I volunteer for stuff at church because I don't want Pastor Allen to think I'm a jerk.

But the real blessing is that even knowing all this can't help it. God loves us because Christ died for us—and that makes us—selfish, petty, and poorly motivated though we may be—special in his eyes.   SS

Jealousy (Monday)

"But on Cain and his offering [the Lord] did not look with favor. So Cain was very angry, and his face was downcast" (Gen. 4:5).

Since the beginning of time, jealousy has been a problem. We all worry about how we come off in comparison to our peers. All of us at times think more of ourselves than others. Like Cain, we become angry when others are chosen over us. Jealousy is a deadly disease infecting us all. We may never be completely cured of it, but we can go to a doctor for help so that it will not take over our lives.

The doctor is Jesus, who died to stop the spread of jealousy and all sin. Knowing that God loves us that much, we don't need to worry about how we come off. Instead, we can be glad for what others have achieved.

AW

God Sees (Tuesday)

"Sin is crouching at your door; it desires to have you, but you must master it" (Gen. 4:7).

God sees sides of us that we don't see.

Cain did the right thing in offering a sacrifice to God, but there was something wrong, and God knew it. Cain looked good, but jealousy and anger were brewing inside him.

Sometimes I try to do something that's right, but it turns out to be a disaster. Then I get angry and down on myself. Later I realize that even though I messed things up, God was still working in me. I didn't look too good, but underneath it all God was giving me the desire to do what was right. And God may even be able to make something good out of it. That's something to be thankful for!

AW

Talk about It   (Wednesday)

"Cain attacked his brother Abel and killed him" (Gen. 4:8).

Why is there so much murder in the world? Could it be because there's not as much communication as there should be? Instead of talking out their problems, people start fights. But this doesn't help; it just creates more problems.

If you find yourself in a situation where you feel aggressive and out of control, first get away and cool down. Then, ask God for help. Instead of violence, Cain should have taken a walk and told God how he felt.

As Christians, if we are angry or have a problem, why not talk to God about it before we do something we'll be sorry for?   AW

Fessing Up   (Thursday)

"Then the Lord said to Cain, 'Where is your brother Abel?'
" 'I don't know,' he replied. 'Am I my brother's keeper?' " (Gen. 4:9).

When God asked Cain where Abel was, Cain lied. Was it because he was afraid to admit that he was jealous and had murdered Cain?

Why is it so hard to admit, even to ourselves, that we are jealous? Perhaps because we picture ourselves above such behavior.

Jealousy can cause us to do some bad things. We may not murder someone, but our jealous words and actions hurt others very deeply. Instead of hiding our jealousy, we can be open about it with God in prayer. Maybe then the jealousy will fade away, and love can take its place.

AW

Alone (Friday)

"I will be a restless wanderer on the earth, and whoever finds me will kill me" (Gen. 4:14).

Cain's punishment banished him from the things he knew and loved best. He felt alone on the earth and feared the revenge of others. But he was wrong in thinking that God had entirely left him. God's mark of protection would go with him.

Sometimes when we goof things up and find ourselves facing a new or unwanted situation, we feel just as alone as Cain. In our guilt we feel separated from others and wonder if God himself hasn't given up on us.

But like Cain, we have a mark that stays with us forever. We are eternally marked with the image of Jesus. We can know his forgiveness and start anew. We are still his.   AW

God Cares for Us (Saturday)

" 'If anyone kills Cain, he will suffer vengeance seven times over.' Then the Lord put a mark on Cain so that no one who found him would kill him" (Gen. 4:15).

When Cain killed Abel, God didn't have to forgive him or let him have another chance. God could have decided that Cain was a hopeless sinner, and could either have killed him or let someone else do the job. But God had mercy on Cain, and put a protective mark on him.

All of us have done some terrible things. God doesn't have to forgive us or let us have another chance. Fortunately, we have a loving God to talk to, a God who forgives us. We carry the marks of sin, but we are also forgiven.   AW

Week 37   Mark 14:27-31,66-72
Denial (Sunday)

Sometimes the toughest among us are just as likely to falter under stress. Everyone has a breaking point, and almost everyone has a private fear that may become a part of that breaking point.

Toward the end of George Orwell's futuristic novel *1984* the hero is tortured by the thought police in order to straighten out his thinking. He resists quite well until they discover he is deathly afraid of rats. He confesses, recants, even betrays his girlfriend to keep them from putting a hungry rat against his face.

Peter boasted that he could remain faithful: "Even if all fall away, I will not." Jesus tried to set him straight. "Before the rooster crows twice you yourself will disown me three times," Jesus said. Peter couldn't believe it. "Even if I have to die with you, I will never disown you."

Peter did disown Jesus. He cussed and swore up and down that he didn't even know him. The rooster crowed. Peter wept bitterly.

We all deny our Lord in small and large ways. The little denials come on us so fast we scarcely recognize them. Someone vainly says "Oh, God!" and we don't complain. Maybe those words slip past our own lips. Someone complains about the faith or the church, and we don't stand up for it.

Our larger denials come at times of doubt, when we sink into a quagmire and wonder if this whole business of God and Jesus and heaven and being saved is all hogwash.

Fortunately for most of us, the small slips don't happen that often, and the large denials don't last long. The beauty of our faith is that denials, large and small, can be forgiven. Peter's were.   SS

No Need to Fear Death (Monday)

"But after I have risen, I will go ahead of you into Galilee" (Mark 14:28).

When the crowd turned against Jesus, Peter thought that he would be alone if Jesus were killed. He didn't understand that Jesus would rise from the dead and return to his disciples on earth before going to heaven. Peter ran from danger, not realizing the meaning that Jesus' death would have for him.

From our point in time, we don't have the uncertainty that Peter had. We know that Jesus conquered death for himself and for us, making death the passageway to eternal life. We can be at peace, knowing we don't need to fear leaving this world. Jesus is waiting for us.   JS

Beware of Boasting (Tuesday)

"Peter declared, 'Even if all fall away, I will not' " (Mark 14:29).

Shocked, Jeff read the letter again. "This must be a mistake," he said to himself. But there it was on paper, "You have not been accepted into Stanford."

Jeff was debate captain, class president, and a 4.0 student. He had told his friends, relatives—even his parents' friends—that he would be attending Stanford next fall. What would he tell them now?

Peter was also outspoken in his confidence. In front of the other disciples he promised Jesus he would never deny him, yet later that night he did.

Like Jeff and Peter, we all fail at times, so we should be careful not to loudly proclaim our abilities. Let's lead our lives with *quiet* confidence.   JS

Forgive as We Have Been Forgiven (Wednesday)

"Before the rooster crows twice you yourself will disown me three times" (Mark 14:30).

Jesus knew beforehand that Peter would deny him, yet he did not become angry and reject Peter. Instead, he was sad, gentle, and forgiving.

How do we act when our friends hurt us? We usually get mad and yell at them or, at the other extreme, we refuse to speak to them. Sometimes we even plan how to hurt them in return.

It is difficult to forgive someone who has hurt us, but as Christians we should try. When it seems impossible to forgive, we can remember the countless times we have been forgiven by God. The Holy Spirit helps us follow Jesus' example. We forgive others as he has forgiven us.

JS

Who's Right? (Thursday)

"Even if I have to die with you, I will never disown you" (Mark 14:31).

We will probably never be called to risk our lives for our beliefs as Peter was, but we may be called to witness for Christ at the expense of our popularity.

As teenagers, we face many choices. Should we drink? do drugs? have sex? cheat? drive recklessly? vandalize? gossip? Sometimes we think, "It doesn't hurt anything, and everyone else is doing it." But if we have doubts as to whether an action is right or wrong, we should ask Christ what he wants us to do. Does he want us to accept the beer and get drunk, or to be in control of our actions?

The love of God leads us to please God and follow God's will rather than our own personal desires or the questionable actions of popular "friends."

JS

Following the Crowd (Friday)

"I do not know this man of whom you speak" (Mark 14:71).

Since the start of high school, Amy had quit spending time with Dawn. Amy's new friends didn't think Dawn dressed or acted right. Amy felt bad for ignoring Dawn, but she didn't want to lose her new friends.

When people mocked Jesus and threatened to kill him, Jesus' friend Peter swore he did not know Jesus. Although he loved Jesus and knew he should not deny him, Peter did not want to endanger himself.

Both Amy and Peter put themselves ahead of their friends. Amy was afraid of being unpopular; Peter was afraid of bodily harm. Yet they both felt guilty about the choices they made.

Should we obey our conscience, or should we succumb to peer pressure? JS

Hope after Hopelessness (Saturday)

"And [Peter] broke down and wept" (Mark 14:72).

"What have I done?" moaned Peter. His chest felt as if it had caved in. He had left Jesus to face the tauntings of the crowd alone. *If only I had one more chance!* Peter thought. *Then I would stay by Jesus to the end—even if it means death.*

We have all wished we could turn back time. How convenient it would be to erase words or actions we are ashamed of and which make us feel sad and guilty.

Peter's sadness overpowered him. He hated himself and did not know how he could go on. But with God's healing forgiveness Peter lifted his head and continued his Christian walk. He even became the solid rock of the church.

We, too, can find God's strength in our weakest moments. JS

Week 38   Psalm 23

In the Presence of My Enemies (Sunday)

When Jack blew the whistle on his friends, he knew there would be trouble, but he never thought it would have lasted this long. No one went to jail over it, but they were put on probation and had to pay back every penny.

Not one of them would talk to Jack, even now, a year later. It hadn't been easy. There was something like a fight about a month after the trial. Jack defended himself, but didn't really fight back. One of his car tires was slit in the school parking lot too. He suspected his former friends—but couldn't prove anything, of course.

If he had it to do over, Jack knew he would do the same thing. They came and tried to sell Jack the equipment at about half its value. He knew something was wrong. He asked, and they just hemmed and hawed. But when he later saw the list of the stolen equipment, he knew where they had gotten it.

Jack told his father, his father told the police, and the legal proceedings began. The police protected Jack's identity fairly well, but his friends guessed:

"You squealed on us, didn't you?"

"Who says I did?"

"No one else really knew it."

There was a long pause. Jack finally spoke. "Yes, I did. What you did was wrong, and you knew it."

"We'll get you," one of them said. They did, too.

Several times in the lunchroom, when he sat near one of them, Jack thought of Psalm 23, "You prepare a table before me in the presence of my enemies." They used to be friends. Too bad. Jack would do it again, though. Right was right.   SS

Someone Who Cares (Monday)

"The Lord is my shepherd" (Ps. 23:1).

Worthless. That's how my parents make me feel at times. Why don't they leave me alone? I am capable of doing things myself. Why do they keep watching over me? I need to be independent. I want to accomplish something on my own. It's the only way I can become an adult. I'm old enough to take care of myself.

Growing up isn't easy. I am going through a lot of difficult times trying to make people believe in me. Yet there are many times when I'm glad I'm not all alone in the world. When my car breaks down, dad is there to lend a hand. When I can't figure out how to get the zipper in my new dress, mom rushes to my aid. When I'm sick, they are there. It really is good to have someone who cares.   JJS

A Slice of Bread (Tuesday)

"I shall lack nothing" (Ps. 23:1).

In psychology class we learned about an interesting event that occurred immediately after the Second World War. The Allied armies gathered together many hungry, homeless children and placed them in large camps to care for them. However, at night they did not sleep well and seemed restless and afraid.

Finally a psychologist hit upon a solution. After the children were put to bed they each were given a slice of bread to hold. The slice of bread produced marvelous results. The children went to sleep, subconsciously feeling they would have something to eat the next day. That assurance gave the children a peaceful rest.

God has provided well for me today and he will again tomorrow. There is no need to be anxious.   JJS

Digesting Life (Wednesday)

"He makes me lie down in green pastures" (Ps. 23:2).

While visiting my friend Nancy's farm, I discovered an interesting fact about sheep. About 30 sheep were lying down in the pasture one afternoon. They all seemed to be chewing something, yet they were not biting at the grass that surrounded them. Nancy informed me that sheep, like cows, take time to lie down and chew their cud. This is nature's way of digestion for them.

We teenagers live very busy lives. We work and play with abandon and surround ourselves with records and radios. Our quiet moments for rest and reflection are often few and far between. Yet our busy Lord often took time to be alone to pray. We also need times when we can turn aside and digest life. JJS

Getting Back on Track (Thursday)

"He restores my soul" (Ps. 23:3).

The story of David fascinates me. God helped him defeat the giant Goliath. God led David to be a mighty general and a successful, righteous king. But son David got busy and felt self-important. He had a loyal soldier killed so he could have the man's wife. His burden of guilt became too heavy to bear. In his misery he turned to God in repentance, and God heard, forgave, and restored him.

Like an orange that has had the juice squeezed out of it, our lives can become empty shells without the Spirit of God to revive us. What joy there is when we get back on track in our Christian lives and let God restore us and lead us in his righteous paths! JJS

Walking through the Valley (Friday)

"Even though I walk through the valley of the shadow of death, I will fear no evil" (Ps. 23:4).

Walking through a large, dark parking lot in a large city filled with crime is not my idea of fun. I keep thinking to myself that this is not the place to be alone. It's strange how many different noises you can hear in an empty parking lot and how you can imagine that someone is sneaking up behind you. But when you want to get home after work, you sometimes have to walk through the darkness alone.

Facing the reality of death in this world can be a terrifying experience. No one cares to walk that dark valley alone. That's why I'm glad I'm a Christian. Wherever I walk, God goes with me. His loving hands protect me. I never am really all alone.   JJS

I Like That House (Saturday)

"I will dwell in the house of the Lord forever" (Ps. 23:6).

I am a P.K. (preacher's kid). Because of my father's work we have moved every few years, and I have lived in a number of different houses.

One of my favorites was a brand-new split-level house with a large family room, game room, and sliding doors onto a nice deck. We moved from that new parsonage to a house which was almost a hundred years old. It had bats in the attic, snakes in the basement, and mice in the kitchen. It was, however, located in a beautiful country setting.

I have discovered that any house is home when you live there in love with your family and friends. I don't know much about heaven, but I know I'll love it because Jesus and my family and friends will be there.   JJS

Week 39   Matthew 8:23-27
Stilling a Storm (Sunday)

Marv was in the back seat. His niece was sleeping, her head on his shoulder. His brother-in-law was at the controls. His sister was in the other front seat beside him. They were indeed flying, but from the window it looked more as if they were submerged in a sea of gray.

"This is what I was afraid of," his brother-in-law said, straining to see ahead of him. "We have all the instruments we need, but this is no fun at all."

No fun! Marv would surely describe their flight in more negative terms than that. They were heading home from a weekend trip. It looked now as if they should have driven—or not come at all.

Marv looked down at his niece. She was sleeping through the whole thing, just as Jesus slept through the storm in the back of the boat. The disciples had been worried too. "Lord, save us! We're going to drown!" they yelled.

Marv wondered if the Lord cared what was happening to their plane. He wished Jesus was there to still the storm. He wished he *himself* had such power. He leaned forward and patted his sister on the shoulder. She reached up and patted his hand with her own. It was supposed to be a reassuring pat, but it didn't work.

Marv closed his eyes to pray, "Get us out of this," he prayed over and over. He kept that up for maybe five minutes. The engine hummed along all the while, as if the weather were no problem at all.

"Well, well," his brother-in-law said.

Marv opened his eyes, discontinuing his prayer. They had broken out of the overcast. As far as you could see ahead, the sky was clear. Unlimited visibility. Jesus once again had stilled a storm.

"Looks as if we flew out of it," his sister said.

The Comforting Weight (Monday)

"A furious storm came up on the lake" (Matt. 8:24).

Outside the tent camper, the storm was howling. The fold-down table that served as a bed for my parents was on the same end of the camper where my two brothers slept. My end overlooked a stream.

The wind was rocking my end of the camper far up into the air. I was only eight or nine at the time, so there wasn't much weight on my side. I was screaming and crying, terrified that we were going to be tossed into the "huge river." Then my father came to my side and lay down, the weight of his body keeping the camper from jerking until the storm was over.

In the same way, our Lord will protect us with the weight of his power until the storms that frighten us are stilled. EMB

My Sky Was Black (Tuesday)

". . . the waves swept over the boat" (Matt. 8:24).

My sky was black; the air turned cool.
The fierce wind howled and seemed so cruel.
The rain, it soaked me to the bone.
I felt that I was all alone.

Then like the Twelve upon that day,
I came to know along the way
the answer to the storm in me—
so much like theirs upon the sea—
was knowing I'll be safe and warm
as Jesus calms my every storm. EMB

The One Who Calms (Wednesday)

"The disciples went and woke him" (Matt. 8:25).

When three friends and I took a canoe into a shallow stream, I became uneasy. The canoe was riding a little low for my taste, and one of our paddlers was leaning to the side, saying how much fun it is to tip canoes. He was really testing my faith in him!

The disciples also felt uneasy while they were in the storm. Their boat was bigger than a canoe, but their sea was larger than a shallow stream. I didn't think the canoe would tip, and even if it did, I didn't have far to swim. The disciples, on the other hand, felt they were in great danger. They hurried to wake Jesus, and he calmed the sea as well as their fears.

Sometimes, in spite of our faith, fears do arise, but Jesus can calm both seas and our fears.   EMB

God Is Better than a Teddy Bear (Thursday)

"And it was completely calm" (Matt. 8:26).

Graham is a very worn-out, tired-looking teddy bear. We've been through many storms as I've been growing up, and Graham has received the brunt of several tantrums. There have also been many nights I've hugged him close while crying myself to sleep. Graham listened tirelessly to all my little-girl complaints. I could tell Graham anything, and my secrets were safe. But, try as he might, Graham could never really do anything to help solve the problem.

God is better than a teddy bear, because we can bring him "grown-up" storms, and somehow, he will help. After all, Jesus endured the cross, the ultimate humiliation that makes all our "grown-up" problems assume the size of those Graham heard. He can help us endure all our problems—no matter what the size.   EMB

The Storm Within (Friday)

"You of little faith, why are you so afraid?" (Matt. 8:26).

I sometimes feel as if there is a storm raging within me, as my fears, pains, confusion, insecurities, and sometimes even hatred all merge into one forceful gale. At these times, when I call out "Save me, Lord! I am perishing," I can't understand why Jesus leaves me alone to face the storm.

When the hurricane dies down, a quiet strength creeps in. Jesus hasn't really left me alone. He has calmed the waves that faith wasn't enough to beat. My daily battle with sin is not a battle I must fight alone. I know that with each storm Jesus and I weather together, my faith will grow stronger. If you weather every storm with Jesus, you will find your faith growing stronger too!   EMB

Personal Miracles (Saturday)

"What kind of man is this? Even the winds and the waves obey him!" (Matt. 8:27).

The disciples had been with Jesus for quite a while and had seen him perform many miracles. Yet they were awestruck when he calmed the storm, because this miracle touched them personally.

Miracles go on about us everyday. Every morning the sun comes up, and every evening the moon comes up. Babies are born every day. These and others are daily phenomena we often take for granted. It is only as one takes time to watch a particularly beautiful sunset, or a baby brought into the family, that the full impact of the miracle hits, for it involves one personally. Sometimes it takes a miracle to touch us personally before we realize that Jesus is more than a mere man; he is our own personal Savior.   EMB

Week 40   Esther 3–6
Saved from Persecution (Sunday)

The story of Mordecai is the story of a program or persecution that didn't happen. The words of Haman's decree sound a lot like something Hitler might have written 2500 years later:

> There is a certain people dispersed and scattered among the peoples in. . . your kingdom, who keep themselves separate. Their customs are different. . . and they do not obey the king's laws. . . . If it pleases the king, let a decree be issued to destroy them.

Reading this section of Esther brings to mind the mounds of emaciated bodies being buried by bulldozers at Buchenwald and Dachau. Further visions come of the walking dead with their clothes hanging loosely on their starved bodies, their sunken, staring eyes scarcely seeing. We ask ourselves how humans could do such things to other humans. Prejudice, carried to its logical conclusions, is monstrous.

But Esther's part in this story reminds us of the best in human unselfishness. When Esther risks her life, doing an unlawful thing to try to stop the persecution, she sounds noble indeed:

> I will go to the king, even though it is against the law. And if I perish, I perish.

We are reminded of the stories of Corrie ten Boom, of Anne Frank, of Raoul Wallenberg. They were resisters. There were those who would not let their prejudices be roused, who would not do what they knew was evil.

We need constantly to be on guard against prejudice. Prejudice worms its way into the very fabric of our lives, denying and destroying the very best that Christ came to teach us: "Love your neighbor as yourself."   SS

You Can't Judge a Book (Monday)

"Their customs are different from those of all other people" (Esther 3:8).

Bob clenched his fist. "I'm gonna knock yer head off, Eskimo!" he bellowed. "You're funny, and I'm not laughing. You don't belong here."

"Wait!" yelped Lou. Before Bob could reply, Lou had a piece of string looped around his hands. Bob's eyes narrowed. He'd never seen a cat's cradle. But before long they were busy with the game, each enjoying and learning about the other.

Like Bob, we sometimes see people who act or look differently as actually *being* different. We shouldn't hurt—mentally or physically—people who appear different. We all have something to learn from each other. We are all one under God.   DW

Use Your Blanket (Tuesday)

"Mordecai. . . went out into the city, wailing loudly and bitterly" (Esther 4:1).

When I came home from a fishing trip and learned that my dog had died, I was wrecked. I gave a loud and bitter cry to equal Mordecai's. But I didn't cry forever. Eventually I got up and began life again. One of the things that helped lift me, besides the fact that I would have gotten pretty hungry lying on the ground, was my faith in God.

Faith is more than just a term for something you feel. Faith is ever-present, always reliable. Faith helped pull Mordecai and me through our times of trouble, and it will do the same for you if you give it the chance.   DW

Go to the King (Wednesday)

"He told him to urge her to go into the king's presence to beg for mercy and plead with him for her people" (Esther 4:8).

"Prayer is *not* cool, mom," Dan said as he left.

"Prayer is *not* cool." He was talking with Bill in the locker room. Bill was a junior and Dan idolized him.

"Hey, I don't know," replied Bill. "I prayed for my dad when he was dying, and every once in awhile I'll pray about something."

Dan was amazed. "But how can—"

"Hey. They call God the King, don't they?"

"Yeah, well—"

"That means king over everybody, even us. And it might do you some good to pray. God's there to help us."

"Oh," Dan said.   DW

The Sign (Thursday)

"And who knows but that you have come to royal position for such a time as this?" (Esther 4:14).

Tom paced a few steps to the left, then the right. "I don't know what to do!" he shouted.

Tom had just moved to the new school, and yesterday he saw two older kids break his class's science project. Tom thought of telling who did it, but that might make somebody mad at him. Tom also thought of continuing to try to fit in and forgetting that the incident ever happened.

Like Tom, we often come to a fork in the road, and must choose between what we know will "save" us, and what we know is right. God watches and guides us. We can look to him for help in our choice as we look to a sign pointing us on the right path.   DW

Something Will Be Done (Friday)

"Nothing has been done for him" (Esther 6:3).

Harry walked home from school. His little sister walked with him. Harry took out the trash. His sister ate a donut and let the crumbs fall on the floor. Harry's father came in, told his sister that she's a "good kid," and went back outside. He missed Harry, somehow.

Harry's probably thinking, "It's OK. I'll come out on top in the end because I'm the better kid." You and I, in similar situations, have no doubt had similar thoughts. But we can't be sure where we'll come out "in the end." We *can* reassure ourselves with this: if nothing has been done for us right away, something will be done later. God loves us all, and that love evens the score.   DW

Sheila the Great (Saturday)

"Whom is there that the king would rather honor than me?" (Esther 6:6).

Sheila strode into her room, full of praise. "I'm the best, and everyone knows it," she said. She caught her eye in the mirror. "Ah, I am beautiful!" she crooned. She spun on one heel. "My heels can do magic!" She waltzed out of her bedroom. "What a wonderful walk I have!" She glanced downward. "And my legs! So perfectly sculptured." She was enjoying her legs so much that she didn't see the stairs. "I tumble so agilely!" she screeched as she fell. She came to earth quickly. "Hmmmm," she said. "Maybe pride *does* go before a fall."

We fall often, and as gracelessly as Sheila. But God's grace is there to lift us to our feet.   DW

Week 41   Acts 17:16-34
To an Unknown God (Sunday)

Just like the people of Athens, Mike worshiped an unknown god. His friend Paul marveled at the way Mike lived. He was honest, he never swore or told dirty jokes, he could always be trusted, he was a superb friend. Mike was a fine young man in every way.

One day in the youth group, Paul and some others were discussing with the pastor what the ideal young Christian would be like. They all chipped in some ideas, building up this hypothetical Christian superperson.

When they were through, the pastor asked, "Is there anyone like that in this town?" They thought about it for a while, then Paul said, "My friend Mike."

Some of them laughed. There were a few incredulous comments: "Baloney." "No way." "Not him."

They got to discussing Mike and how he lived. Some of them asked if he had any religion at all. Paul, who knew him best, had to admit he didn't. But his actions were more Christ-like than those of anybody else they knew.

The pastor opened his Bible to the story of Paul at Athens. "Your friend Mike," the pastor said, "sounds a lot like the Athenians. He worships an unknown god. I think we owe it to him to make God known to him. All he needs is a faith."

"You mean," Paul said, "that he wouldn't have to change the way he acts, only he way he believes."

"That's precisely it," the pastor said. "We could give him a reason for living the good life. Let's start this spring. How about it, Paul? Could we start maybe with my meeting him? Could you arrange that?"

"I guess so," Paul said. "Sure, I could."   SS

Going Places (Monday)

"The God who made the world and everything in it is the Lord of heaven and earth and does not live in temples built by hands" (Acts 17:24).

With the Lord in your life
You can go up the wall,
    or down the line,
    over your budget,
    or under your size,
    across the country,
    or around the world,
    off your rocker,
    or on your deathbed,
And he will always be there to help.   KK

The Gift (Tuesday)

"From one man he made every nation of men. . ." (Acts 17:26).

I've traveled our country, I've been far and wide,
from top to bottom and side to side.
Wherever I go, as I walk with my feet,
I'm always surprised by the people I meet.

People all over, the short and the tall,
some with big noses and others with small,
various hobbies as well as religions,
differing races and different decisions,

—all are the same in a good many ways.
One person sells, and another one pays.
Christ Jesus, he died so that each one could live.
There's nothing at all that our Lord didn't give.   KK

When I See Jesus (Wednesday)

"He is not far from each one of us" (Acts 17:27).

When I see only darkness,
Jesus gives light.
When I'm stuck on the ground,
Jesus gives flight.
If I feel like I'm losing,
Jesus gives gain.
If I see only stubble,
Jesus gives grain.
When I'm ready to fall,
Jesus gives rope.
When my life brings me sorrow,
Jesus gives hope.   KK

You Never Give Up (Thursday)

"For in him we live and move and have our being" (Acts 17:28).

It's fun to go buy a new outfit,
but I still owe the club for my dues.
I don't like to go see the dentist,
but I'm glad when she gives me good news.

I'd rather not eat my asparagus,
or spend the day mowing the lawn.
I wish they would give me less homework,
and on and on and on.

No matter what time or what day,
there's some place I'd rather not be.
But Jesus, you never give up,
and I thank you for still loving me!   KK

All You Have to Do (Friday)

"In the past God overlooked such ignorance, but now he commands all people everywhere to repent" (Acts 17:30).

I said to God,
  "I don't want to be a Christian.
  All you have to do
    —like go to church on Sunday,
    and smile at old ladies,
    and stop picking on your sister,
    and mow the lawn free for your grandma,
    and never have "too much" fun—
  All you have to do
  is too much for me."

God said to me,
  "All you have to do
  is ask."

KK

Crowd (Saturday)

"Now when they heard about the resurrection of the dead, some of them sneered" (Acts 17:32).

The CROWD thought
  Noah's story wouldn't hold water,
  Sodom was a nice little place to settle down.
The CROWD thought
  Chris Columbus hadn't been around enough,
  Joan of Arc ought to spend more time cooking.
The CROWD thought
  it would be smooth sailing for the *Titanic*,
  six million Jews were a nuisance.
The CROWD thinks
  it can get along without Jesus.
What do YOU think?

KK

Week 42   Psalm 91
The Terror of the Night (Sunday)

The psalmist expressed his trust in God for every kind of comfort, refuge, and protection—among them the terrors of the night.

So many of our fears are terrors of the night—unseen horrors. Spooky movies exploit this. We don't mind being frightened when we have paid for it, when we are scrunched down into a theater seat and the fear is controlled, when there is no *real* danger.

We probably aren't as frightened of our unseen fears as our ancestors were. Before electric lights, fears began at the edge of the campfire's glow or just outside the massive bolt on the oaken door. There were trolls, hobgoblins, and spooks of every kind lurking in every darkness.

You may remember those fears when you were little. Something was in the closet or moving around in the corner of your dark room. When the fears would get too consuming, you would cry, mom or dad would come in, switch on the light, and assure you that all was well—no spooks, ghosts, or lurking dangers.

Those fears don't all disappear as we grow up. Some of them persist. Some have real basis. There *are* dangers in the night—muggers, rapists, thieves. But most of our terrors of the night are just baseless fears.

Like the good parent he is, God can snap on the light for us and free us from our nameless terrors, from things that go bump in the night. We put ourselves in his hands. We need only trust in his care and protection, like the psalmist of old.   SS

Teach Us to Pray (Monday)

"He will call upon me, and I will answer him" (Ps. 91:15).

Jesus' disciples never asked him for the power to perform miracles or for the intellectual ability to influence crowds. But they did say, "Lord, teach us to pray." They knew that the strength Jesus exhibited in his personal life was nurtured by prayer—communication with his Father.

The Bible says to pray "without ceasing"; prayer is not just folding our hands and bowing our heads, but rather how we approach all of life. How, though, should prayer be approached? ACTS is one method—A for adoration, C for confession, T for thanksgiving, S for supplication. The next four devotions will explore these four aspects of prayer.   KL

Words of Adoration (Tuesday)

"I will say of the Lord, 'He is my refuge and my fortress; my God, in whom I trust' " (Ps. 91:2).

According to the ACTS scheme, the first aspect of prayer is *adoration*. Beginning our prayer with an expression of love and praise for our Lord serves as a reminder of God's goodness and grace. Our prayers are given and received in a loving relationship.

Finding the words to express our love for God is often difficult, though. Reading psalms is an excellent way to learn words of adoration—"How great is your constant love for me! You have saved me from the grave itself. . . . You, O Lord, are a merciful and loving God, always patient, always kind and faithful" (Ps. 86:13,15).   KL

To Forgive and Be Forgiven (Wednesday)

"Surely he will deliver you. . . from the deadly pestilence" (Ps. 91:3).

The second part of prayer in ACTS is *confession.* Healing and renewal of life begin with cleansing the mind of guilt from sin. Guilt's "solvent" is forgiveness. Forgiveness, however, rests on confession—owning up to sin and requesting forgiveness, both human and divine.

To experience forgiveness is to break the barriers erected in human relationships—barriers that also separate us from God. Reconciliation can take place once those barriers are torn down with prayers of confession. To forgive and to be forgiven—the crux of prayers of confession.   KL

Thanks for Everything (Thursday)

"I will deliver him and honor him" (Ps. 91:15).

The third part of prayer in ACTS is *thanksgiving.* The Bible reminds us to give God thanks for all things and in all circumstances.

Thanksgiving focuses on the things we have rather than what we haven't. A "thanksgiving list" reveals more pluses than minuses in life.

Thanksgiving also focuses on God's goodness. The positive aspects of a negative situation become visible.

Thirdly, giving thanks for answered prayers builds confidence and trust in God. Even the *no* answer may have been ultimately beneficial. Though it may be difficult, we ought to give thanks for *everything!*   KL

For Our Needs and the Needs of Others (Friday)

"I will protect him, for he acknowledges my name." (Ps. 91:14).

The final part of prayer in ACTS is *supplication.* Offering prayers of adoration, confession, and thanksgiving prepares us to ask God for the things we desire and pray for the needs of others. Whether God's answer will be "yes," "no," or "wait awhile," we can in faith pray, "Your will, not my will, be done."

Faith in Jesus, made strong by prayer, helps us realize from whom our blessings come. Faith sustains us through bad times also, enabling us to see the ever-present light and hope in the world—Jesus. He promises, "I will be with you always, to the end of the age" (Matt. 28:20 TEV).   KL

Dave and the Angel (Saturday)

"For he will command his angels concerning you to guard you in all your ways; they will lift you up in their hands, so that you will not strike your foot against a stone" (Ps. 91:11-12).

"Help! Is anybody up there?" Dave shouted as he dangled over the edge of the cliff, enveloped in a thick fog. He had no idea how far he might fall if he let go of the tree root that he clutched.

"Dave, I was sent by the Lord to save you," said a voice high above him. "Do you believe the Lord Almighty can save you?"

"Yes, I do! Save me!" Dave cried, his strength ebbing.

"Then let go of the tree root, Dave, because there's a rock ledge only four feet below you. Trust me."

"Is *anybody else* up there?" Dave pleaded.   KL

Week 43 John 13:1-20
The Lowliest Slave (Sunday)

The disciples couldn't understand it, especially Peter. The footwasher in a first-century household was the lowliest slave of all—and was usually useless for any other work.

The footwashing slave was someone to ignore. You would pay about as much attention to him then as we do to a pop machine now. He did a job you appreciated, especially after a long journey on a dusty road, but you didn't pat him on the head, or praise him, or say "Oh my, that feels good." You simply chatted with your host as your feet were being washed, and took the washing as your due.

That's why the disciples were so shocked at Jesus. His public ministry was almost over, and by a gentle ongoing miracle many of the disciples were beginning to see who he really was. He was Lord; he was Master; he was King. Hadn't the crowd, afterall, just last Sunday, treated him to a royal entry procession?

Now here he was, on his knees, washing feet. Impetuous Peter said, "You shall *never* wash my feet." Peter didn't understand. Jesus was putting on a little one-act play. He was acting out the role of servant—not servanthood in soothing, socially acceptable, comfortable modes, but servanthood of the lowliest, most shameful, and most thankless kind.

All this to teach us a lesson: "Now that I, your Lord and Teacher, have washed your feet, you also should wash one another's feet." Not necessarily wash feet—but help, care, love, reach out to the hopeless. In those ways we wash feet—and obey Christ's command.   SS

Apostle Number One (Monday)

"Jesus knew. . . that he had come from God and was returning to God" (John 13:3).

Gentle, Lord! Such holy hands to touch my feet. Don't let your holiness burn them. Shield me.

Don't you see the dirt between my toes and under my toenails? And the calluses and the wart?

I look into your eyes and cannot bear your gaze, but I understand.

"I know who I am," your eyes say. "I know where I have come from and where I am going. I come from God and will go to him."

Yes! Your identity does not come from us or what *we* think of you, but from what *God* thinks. And God is the holiest and greatest of all! So you are free to wash feet.

Teach me that freedom, too, Lord.   PAF

Apostle Number Two (Tuesday)

"Unless I wash you, you have no part with me" (John 13:8).

Jesus is strange. Here he is, the Son of God, one worthy of great honor and glory, washing feet! You'd think he was a slave or something. I mean, really! *We* should be washing *his* feet.

But, come to think of it, Jesus has been like this all along. He's healed people, fed people, taught people. Maybe it's a hint. Maybe that's what Jesus is all about, what makes him great—he serves, he gives, he fulfills needs.

So if I'm going to follow him, I let him serve *me*, let him wash *my* feet. If I do not do that, I reject him and all he's done.   PAF

Enough (Wednesday)

"Not just my feet but my hands and my head as well"
(John 13:9).

This tongue has sinned—
again.
"Tell me more," some say.
Others frown and turn away.
"Please,
cut out
my tongue,"
I say, the final authority.
"No," says God.
"I can make you gentle and loving of speech.
It will be my joy.
I have washed you.
Enough."   PAF

Disneyland (Thursday)

"Now that I, your Lord and Teacher, have washed your
feet, you also should wash one another's feet" (John
13:14).

Donna stood up and yelled for the bus driver to stop.
"What are you doing?" I whispered.

"I'm not going to Disneyland to waste $40 when that
man's walking around with rags tied to him for pants,"
she answered, pointing.

When we reached him, Donna said, "My friend and I
were going to Disneyland, but when I saw you, I realized
how criminal that was. If you'll accept our gift, we'll buy
you some food and clothes."

I just wondered how we'd get home now.

The old man smiled. "God bless you, children!"

"He has, sir. That's why we can help *you*."   PAF

Teresa (Friday)

"You also should wash one another's feet" (John 13:14).

Our youth group sat in a circle, feet bare, trying not to laugh. "I want you to wash the feet of the people here whom you need to forgive or be forgiven by," our pastor had just said.

Teresa went first. She washed everyone's feet. No one really liked her, and I had led the group in teasing her. When she got to me, I realized she had every right to hate me and not wash my feet. But she washed them very carefully. She was forgiving me!

When it was my turn to wash, I washed Teresa's feet, no one else's. I wanted to show her I'd understood. She smiled. I'd never tease her again.   PAF

Wait a Second! (Saturday)

"No servant is greater than his master" (John 13:16).

Jesus fed thousands.
   "No," I tell the Mexican woman and her eight
     starving children, and eat my potato chips.
Jesus touched the lepers, the crippled, the sick.
   I turn my head and joke.
Jesus forgave prostitutes.
   I stare and shake my head from my air-conditioned
     car.
Jesus taught in the streets and from boats.
   I stay silent, opening my mouth only to criticize those
     who do speak out.
Teacher and Lord, who's greater?
   What a lie to think it's me!
   You are God; I am dust.
   Send a revolution through me!   PAF

Week 44   Genesis 42–45

Brotherly Love—and Hate (Sunday)

Joseph's story is superb. I hope you have taken time to read it. Take even more time and go back and start at Chapter 37.

Some of the blame for the bad blood among these brothers certainly belongs to Jacob (also called Israel). Maybe he couldn't help loving Joseph more than the others, but he could have tried to hide that. As it was, he stirred up rivalries and hatred among his sons.

Joseph's early dreams didn't help either. He dreamed he would rule over his older brothers, and he told them so. They were stirred up and plotted to kill him. Reuben counseled restraint. They sold him into slavery instead.

Joseph was a strong and moral young man. He resisted the sexual advances of Potiphar's wife, endured his imprisonment well, and used his brains and abilities with dreams to get back into the king's good graces.

What an amazed bunch of brothers must have stood there as Joseph revealed himself. Were they first fearful for having sold him, then penitent, then thankful?

It was a happy day. Joseph saw the whole thing as God's plan to preserve the remnant, to preserve the children of Israel through seven years of famine. There would be for all time the 12 tribes of Israel that dated back to these 12 sons of Jacob. The forgiving spirit of Joseph made that possible.

This is a story to reread when you are having brother or sister trouble. Many times over the years, the wrong decision would have meant an end to the 12 tribes. Good decisions, and God's hand in the bad ones, saved the family.

No one should lay the saving of your family on you alone, but you *can* help. Learn from Joseph. Learn that forgiveness is what saves a family, that love is stronger than anger, resentment, jealousy, and hatred.   SS

Fishing (Monday)

"Now we must give an accounting for his blood" (Gen. 42:22).

As a fifth grader living in this world of "accounting," I had a hard time understanding the extent of God's forgiveness. I would feel guilty for weeks at the least little thing.

My Sunday school teacher told me something that eased my young mind. "God's forgiveness," she explained, "is like a big lake. The lake is deeper than deep, and wider than wide. When you ask God to forgive your sins, he throws them in this lake. All around the edges of the lake are big signs that say, 'No Fishing!' And I haven't gone "fishing" since!   SD

God's Purpose (Tuesday)

"What is this that God has done to us?" (Gen. 42:28).

She is a beautiful eight-year-old child, full of spunk and energy. Her bright smile reaches out to everyone. She has a chronic disease. Although she will live for many years, her mind and body will soon deteriorate. Her parents ask, "What is this that God has done to us?"

Thousands of years before, in a different situation, Joseph's brothers asked the same questions. In time both Joseph's brothers and the girl's parents found answers. Joseph's brothers and his father were reunited with him again. The young child had brought love and purpose to her parent's lives.

We may find ourselves asking this question. It can be hard to believe God has a reason for everything. Yet, if we will only wait, we will also see God's purpose.   SD

The Youth (Wednesday)

"The men had been seated before him in the order of their ages" (Gen. 43:33).

My eyes moved around the church and focused on a young woman sitting alone. She was about 16 and looked uncomfortable. I'd seen that look in so many young faces. Sadly, young people often don't feel welcome in the church.

This church wasn't seeing some of its most valuable resources—the young people. Most members seemed to assume that anyone under 21 came only because her parents made her. Not this young woman. I could see a fire burning inside her. If someone would let her get involved, she could make a difference. But she was young, so she was left sitting in that back pew.   SD

Good Advice (Thursday)

"So they feasted and drank freely with him" (Gen. 43:34).

Dear Christian Friend,

I've got a problem. My problem is my friends. All they ever want to do is get drunk. They think it's the only way to have fun. I don't think it's for me, but I go along because I don't want to lose my friends. I usually don't drink, but they have really been after me. What should I do?
                                   Confused

Dear Confused,

You have started to answer your own problem. At 16 you've already realized there's more to life. Drinking isn't for you. Stick to your guns! You will find some of your friends respect you for it; the rest you don't need. Things will work out for you in the end. You're not alone.
                            Your Christian Friend
                                        SD

Taking Out the Garbage (Friday)

"And now, do not be distressed and do not be angry with yourselves for selling me here" (Gen. 45:5).

Starting today I will save all the scraps from my meals. I'll pile them in a corner of my room and play with them every day.

That sounds absurd, doesn't it? Yet that is what we do in God's eyes when we continue to worry over our sins. God doesn't want us to dwell on our sins any more than I want to play with garbage. It's hard to accept this. Joseph was trying to tell his brothers not to feel guilty, but to accept forgiveness.

God forgives us completely, if we only ask. If God can forgive us, we can certainly forgive ourselves.   SD

Life's Purpose (Saturday)

"It was to save lives that God sent me ahead of you" (Gen. 45:5).

Lord, your purpose in Joseph's life was so clear. He knew what you wanted from him. I want to do what you want in my life also, but how do I know what that is? I've never had visions or heard voices from heaven. I'm not even sure I have anything to offer you! Sometimes I catch myself doing what I want, not what you want, and other times I can't tell which is which!

I do know that whatever you see in me is yours, Lord. I trust you. Make me the best I can possibly be for you. Thanks!   SD

Week 45   Luke 17:11-19

The Samaritan Comes Back (Sunday)

Once again it's a Samaritan. The one that came back from the 10 healed lepers was a Samaritan. Jesus remarked about it: "Was no one found to return and give praise to God except this foreigner?"

Maybe, all things considered, the return of the Samaritan was predictable. Maybe his thankfulness had a special dimension, considering the healer was a Jew and the healed was a Samaritan. It was highly unlikely that his leprosy could be healed; it was even more unlikely that the miracle of healing should have been performed by a Jew for a Samaritan.

Sometimes the unlikely and unexpected things make us most thankful. When we receive a Christmas or birthday gift from someone from whom we expected nothing, we are particularly thankful.

Or how about the unexpected good grade. You are mystified by your English teacher's essay assignment. You can't really understand what she wants. Time is running out. You sit down and write something so far out and unlike anything you've ever done before that you fully expect an F.

A week later the paper comes back. The grade is A+. There is a short note: "This is *exactly* what I was looking for." She reads your paper to the whole class. You are proud—and thankful.

You are suddenly and unexpectedly in the middle of some sin you never would have dreamed you could commit. You can't believe your own weakness and stupidity. You have nowhere to turn, no one you can tell. You turn to God and you know you are forgiven. You sense it as Christ's renewed presence in your life. You are healed. You are also shown how to get out of your difficulty. You are thankful. Jammed full of thanks.

SS

A Common Need   (Monday)

"Jesus, Master, have mercy on us" (Luke 17:13).

The last of the sandbags was packed firmly in place on top of the wall. Our crew could finally go home and get some needed rest. Taking a last look at the muddy, swirling waters of the flooded river, we lowered our aching bodies from the wall. What a way to spend an Easter vacation! At least our town was safe from the flood.

Our town! We had been so divided. Yet fighting the flood had brought us together. Students and teachers, employers and employees, rich and poor had all worked hard to save our town. We would be a lot closer to one another in the future.

In all the floods of life we need each other and the help of God. Together we cry out for God's mercy.   JJS

Confession Is Good for the Soul (Tuesday)

"Go, show yourselves to the priests" (Luke 17:14).

Linda felt terrible. She had not only drunk too much at a Saturday night party but had given in to her date as well. Several weeks later Linda still felt guilty. She prayed, but she didn't feel forgiven. In desperation she told her best friend Pam.

"There is something else you can do," Pam suggested. "Talk to your minister."

"You mean tell him what I did?" Linda exclaimed.

It took a few days before Linda got up enough nerve to lay her burden before her minister, but the long talk and prayer they had together did wonders for her relationship with God. Linda is thankful for the privilege of confessing her sins to another Christian and receiving the assurance of God's forgiveness.   JJS

Praise the Lord (Wednesday)

"Then one of them, when he saw he was healed, turned back, praising God in a loud voice" (Luke 17:15).

Ten lepers cured of dread disease,
their rotting flesh restored,
their peril past,
good health at last,
when cleansed by our dear Lord.

Just one returned to praise his God.
Just one fell at his feet.
Were not ten blessed?
Where were the rest
to praise His love so so sweet?

You've given me my health, O Lord.
You've made my body strong.
I'll sing your praise
for all my days
in thankfulness and song   JJS

Remember the Giver (Thursday)

"Where are the other nine?" (Luke 17:17).

I looked again with shame at the letter from my grandmother. "Your grandpa and I haven't heard from you for quite a while. I hope you received the birthday gift we sent in the mail." I had indeed received their gift. That nice, crisp $20 bill had delighted me. Could it be that a whole month had gone by and I still hadn't sent them a thank you? I had been busy with school events, but not *that* busy. I just forgot it, that's all. But I had not forgotten to spend the money.

My grandparents mean a lot to me. I must get my priorities straight. From now on I'm going to remember the giver as well as the gift.   JJS

A Little Praise (Friday)

"Was no one found to return and give praise to God?" (Luke 17:18).

"Twenty-five laps around the gym!" the basketball coach shouted.

Sharon was not happy with the thought of more running. She hated running. Playing girl's basketball was fun, but the conditioning part of it was not. Why should she give it her all when she hadn't even received a letter last year?

"Say Sharon, you've really improved on your lay-ups this year. I think your free throws are coming along well too. Keep up the good work," her coach said.

Sharon smiled and started running her laps. Maybe they wouldn't be so bad after all. It was funny what a little praise could do for a person's attitude.   JJS

Trust Him (Saturday)

"Your faith has made you well" (Luke 17:19).

One day when I was growing up, my parents called me in for a serious talk. They told me there was no Santa Claus. That was quite a shock. Even worse, they said there was no Easter bunny either. I had always liked that egg-laying rabbit.

Despite the trauma of losing two close friends in one day, I got over it rather quickly. I discovered others in whom I really could believe. It was amazing to think that my parents loved me enough to place all those gifts under our Christmas tree. I could count on them. They taught me that I could trust deeply in the love of Jesus too. His birth made Christmas exciting. His resurrection made Easter so special. What a joy to be able to trust him with my life!   JJS

Week 46   Psalm 30

Clothed with Joy (Sunday)

When Allen's mother died, he was nearly inconsolable. He hadn't been very close to his father at all. They didn't fight, nor dislike each other, but he had been closest to his mother for as long as he could remember.

Now she was gone, swept away without warning. Who could have predicted so sudden a death? Allen didn't cry at the funeral, and friends and relatives who knew how close they were couldn't understand that. Allen was, in fact, too shocked to hurt. He still couldn't believe she was gone.

The way back was long. It took a year and more. The church helped, and his pastor helped too. Even his father was beginning to sense his moods and needs—indeed, Allen began to understand how lonely his father was, and how much he also had loved his wife, Allen's mother. They had that in common.

The Bible helped a lot. Some passages didn't make sense at first. Like, just a few days after the funeral, Allen read several psalms, among them Psalm 30. When he read the lines, "You turned my wailing into dancing; you removed my sackcloth and clothed me with joy" he just shook his head. "It will never happen," he told himself.

But it did. Not overnight, though. Allen was surprised to find himself first whistling, then singing. The hymns were starting to make sense again. He began to see his mother with God, and happy beyond measure.

He would never stop missing her, but he was working through his grief. And he would learn to be his father's son too.   SS

Blessing from Love (Monday)

"I will exalt you, O Lord, for you lifted me out of the depths" (Ps. 30:1).

When Mary sat down in church and opened her bulletin, she happily noted that one of her favorite hymns would be sung, "How Great Thou Art." After listening to the sermon and participating in the service, she went home with a great joy in her heart. As she recounted all of God's goodness to her, she could only respond, "How great thou art."

Like Mary, you and I have been blessed in so many ways, both materially and spiritually. With the psalmist we can sing, "I will exalt you, O Lord, for you lifted me out of the depths." In Jesus, God has drawn us to himself as a parent hugs a child in a warm embrace. Is it any wonder that Christians love to sing, "How great thou art"?

PJR

Singing Saints (Tuesday)

"Sing to the Lord, you saints of his" (Ps. 30:4).

Have you ever wondered what church services would be like without music? They would be dull and flat, don't you think? Ever since Old Testament times, hymns have been part of worship. The heading of Psalm 30 indicates that it is a song. The psalms were meant to be sung. Over the years, countless lovely hymns have been composed to help God's people praise him.

Music helps us express our innermost feelings, from highest joy to deepest sorrow. St. Paul urged the Ephesians to use "psalms, hymns, and spiritual songs. Sing and make music in your heart to the Lord" (Eph. 5:19).

PJR

O You His Saints (Wednesday)

"Sing to the Lord, you saints of his" (Ps. 30:4).

We often think of saints as people who lived long ago and who performed many heroic deeds for God and for his church. However, in Psalm 30:4 all God's people are called saints. In the New Testament, St. Paul calls all Christians saints. A saint is one who has received Christ's forgiveness. In that sense a saint is holy.

Saints therefore are not just those people we see in the stained-glass windows in churches. They are also people living today. We are saints!

We are not bragging when we call ourselves saints. We did not earn this title; it was given to us because of the death and resurrection of our Lord and Savior, Jesus Christ.   PJR

A Moment, a Lifetime (Thursday)

"For his anger lasts only a moment, but his favor lasts for a lifetime" (Ps. 30:5).

Some people have the idea that in the Old Testament God showed himself as an angry God, but in the New Testament as a loving God. Actually, God is both angry and merciful. His anger, however, lasts "only a moment."

Jesus felt God's full fury when he died on the cross. But God's favor lasts for a lifetime, says the psalmist. God loves us so much that he gave his Son for us. What a comfort it is to know that God's favor (his grace, mercy, love) is with us for a lifetime!

And how long is a lifetime? According to God's plan, our lifetime will never end. We will always live with him, now and forever.   PJR

Weeping and Joy (Friday)

"Weeping may remain for a night, but rejoicing comes in the morning" (Ps. 30:5).

When friends write that they are traveling and plan to stay with you for the night, you may be asked to give up your bed, but you know it is only temporary. They will only "remain for the night."

It is in the firm faith of the psalmist that weeping stays only a little while. Sorrow and pain must give way to the joy that comes with the morning.

Think of Good Friday and Easter. On Friday there was sadness and weeping, but on Easter morning the disciples had joy!

That is our faith too. God promises that he will finally dry all our tears. Filled with God's joy, we can help those who suffer pain now.   PJR

O Lord My God (Saturday)

"O Lord my God, I will give you thanks forever" (Ps. 30:12).

The real beauty in this verse lies in the first person singular possessive pronoun, *my*. What a privilege it is to be so close to God that I can call him *my* God! By calling God "my God," the psalmist is demonstrating the close relationship between oneself and God. Instead of calling God "Divine Sovereign" or "Mighty Creator," we can address him on a personal level. I can call him *my* God!

The Lord's Prayer is a beautiful example of this closeness. Jesus teaches us to pray "*Our* Father." God loves each of us so much that he invites us to say "*my* God," "*our* Father."   PJR

Week 47   Matthew 18:23-25
Big Money (Sunday)

In the margin of my Bible it says a denarius is a *day's* wage and a talent is *15 years'* wages of a laborer. At today's minimum wage, $27 would be a day's earnings. Therefore, 10,000 talents would be 10,000 times $27 times 365 days per year times 15 years or $1,478,250,000. Big money!

Now you may be able to sell John Paul Getty or some other rich person for 1.5 billion dollars, but no king's servant—not then, now now. It wouldn't have helped much to sell them.

Jesus, obviously, wasn't talking about money. He was talking about spiritual things: sin and forgiveness.

Let's just assume that when we read this story, the 1.5 billion is supposed to represent your sin or my sin. Sounds like a lot. But when you pile together every thought, word, and deed, every unkindness, thoughtlessness, and pettiness, every heresy and idiocy and lunacy, every confrontation, lamentation, or machination—if you lump a lifetime of this stuff together, it is quite a lot.

Now if you and I could see all these sins, each one written on a single brick and piled in one pile, it might make quite a monument to our ability to do wrong stuff.

But this parable isn't designed to bury us under a pyramid of our own sin. It is rather to make us thankful for the wonder and the amazement of our forgiveness— and thereby make us more willing and more able—maybe even eager—to forgive others.

Anybody done you any dirt lately? Would it amount to about a denarius' worth—a day's wage? That's not so much, is it? Would it be so hard to forgive it? Sort of, you say? Well, imagine yourself shouting your words of forgiveness from the top of a 1.5 billion dollar brick pile of sin. Easier now? I thought so.   SS

Fear (Monday)

"The kingdom of heaven is like a king who wanted to settle accounts with his servants" (Matt. 18:23).

Erica became afraid. It was not the kind of fear she had when the Internal Revenue Service checked her income, nor was it fear about the people who stopped by her door, asking her to repay their money.

This fear came into Erica's mind as she thought of her debt to God. It could be anything that she had done against the Lord in her life. She realized that she owed God many things. She felt sorry because of her betrayal to God who loved and cared for her so much. What would she do if someday God asked her about the debt?

Erica knew God as the great Forgiver. She promised to repent and hoped that God would forgive her for all the sins she had committed.   THP

The Unforgiving Landlord (Tuesday)

"Be patient with me, and I will pay back everything" (Matt. 18:26).

Trying to restrain his emotion, Hai told me his story: "I came from a rural area which was under the control of my father—a rich, powerful landlord. Life was wonderful until one day a poor farmer came to my dad, begging him to postpone his debt's due date. My father refused. Next day, the poor farmer disappeared. When the former government collapsed, that man returned as a high-ranking revolutionist. He kicked my family off our property and exiled my dad to an unknown place."

"Now I understand what God expects from me, my father, and the others," Hai concluded. "Life is wonderful only if we live each day with forgiveness, love, and care for one another."   THP

Compassion on Christmas Eve (Wednesday)

"The servant's master took pity on him, canceled the debt and let him go" (Matt. 18:27).

The battle had ended a few hours earlier. The gunfire ceased. In the dark sky appeared flares that reminded Van about the seriously wounded guerrilla at his feet.

"Christmas is the time of peace. How come there are only bloodshed and hatred around me?" Van sighed.

"Please forgive me, I had to do what I was told," the man spoke out in pain.

"Could I forgive my most hated enemy? Could I forgive someone who, a short time before, was trying to kill me?" Christmas reminded Van of God who, out of pity and love for humankind, sent his Son into the world to die on a cross so that all might be forgiven.

Several hours later, the man died. And out of his compassion, Van buried the guerrilla's body right where he had fallen and placed a cross on his grave.   THP

A Meaningful Example (Thursday)

"Shouldn't you have had mercy on your fellow servant just as I had on you?" (Matt. 18:33).

"Your aunt came to visit our family last week. She needed money desperately. When she started begging, we almost cried for her difficult situation. So, instead of spending money to take a vacation this year, we decided to lend it to her. Although your sisters agreed with us, they looked very sad. Anyway, we are still more fortunate than many people. God has mercy on our family and gives us more blessings than we deserve, so why shouldn't we share them with others, right, son?"

This was a part of the letter I received from my parents yesterday. My response to them was, "You're definitely right, mom and dad!"   THP

The Forgiving Uncle (Friday)

". . . forgive your brother from your heart" (Matt. 18:35).

My parents were shocked by a letter from my uncle whom they believed was dead since he disappeared five years ago. My mother wept as my dad read it out loud, "Forgive me, brother, for all the wrongs I did to you. After spending a lot of time thinking about my misbehavior, I decided to go into the army. I may see you and your family again if I'm forgiven."

My father was very moved by his brother's letter, and he remembered that God is merciful and always forgives his people for all the wrongs they have done. So my father wrote a forgiving letter to my uncle, insisting that he come back.

"If we can't forget someone's mistakes in the past," my dad said "we're not the true, forgiving Christians God wants us to be."   THP

Brothers and Forgiveness (Saturday)

". . . forgive your brother from your heart" (Matt. 18:35).

I found it hard to forgive my brothers when they hurt my feelings. Whenever they laughed at me, I would find a chance to pay them back. Our relationship became worse because I always tried to get even.

Then, after a Bible study class, I realized that I was acting sinfully toward my brothers, that Jesus wanted me to forgive them as God forgives me and all people. This was a challenge, but through accepting it, my brothers and I gained more understanding of each other. We also learned that forgiving without forgetting is not forgiveness at all. Keeping that in mind, we began building our brotherhood in Christ.   THP

Week 48 Matthew 25:31-46

Starvation in Your Living Room (Sunday)

Maybe the portable TV camera will finally do it. Television is more gruesome than newspaper articles. It now presents us with the emaciated bodies of starving children, their bellies distended, their eyes sunken and dull, sores on their faces, flies feeding on the sores. Hard to ignore.

It is a challenge to us. How will we respond? We need to mobilize for the relief of human suffering.

What can I do? you ask. How can I do anything for the least of these brothers and sisters of Christ? Where can I find some of these starving, these imprisoned, these unclothed and unsheltered ones?

Well, some of them are right in your town and mine. Ask your pastor what agencies do the helping in your town. Volunteer your services. Ask also about the hunger and relief agencies supported by your church. Talk to other youth about fund-raising projects that can go directly to needy areas.

Be a lobbyist at home. You may not have many dollars to invest in helping, but your parents may. Ask them if they would contribute. Many suffering children and adults are helped by church relief agencies. Remind your parents of this important work.

Jesus said, "Whatever you did for one of the least of these. . ." Our littlest decisions to help (or not to help) add up to forever.   SS

Sharing Some Bread (Monday)

"I was hungry and you gave me something to eat" (Matt. 25:35).

When one of our city's homeless came to my pastor's house asking for food, he was told to wait outside while the pastor quickly fixed a plastic bag dinner.

Later, when we were driving by our church, we saw the man eating the food he was just given.

When Pastor Dave shared some of his food, he was helping Jesus. Jesus says that if you feed the hungry, you also feed him. By sharing some of our bread with the needy, we also share the bread of God.   TLM

Opening Our Hearts and Our Homes (Tuesday)

"I was a stranger and you invited me in" (Matt. 25:35).

They didn't know what to do. The young travelers from Spain had come to our city hoping to stay at a downtown hotel, but when they got there, they found out that their reservations had been lost.

With no place to spend the night, their story was broadcast over the news, and within three hours all the travelers had a place to spend the night.

The people who opened up their homes not only shared their homes, but they also opened their hearts and gained new friendships as well.   TLM

Pulling Together to Help (Wednesday)

"I needed clothes and you clothed me" (Matt. 25:36).

A fire in our city recently showed me all the love and caring that was present in our community.

When nine row-houses were destroyed in a fire, a plea went out for clothes, food, and donations to help the victims. Shelters for the homeless were also found. Overwhelmed by the love shown to them, the victims believed that maybe this tragedy was needed to show them the love that actually is present in our community.

By helping them, we also helped Jesus, and Jesus helped us become closer to our neighbors.   TLM

They Had to Ask (Thursday)

"Lord, when. . .?" (Matt. 25:37).

The Lord will come again to judge the living and the dead. He will separate the people into two groups. Those whose faith has produced works of love will go into eternal life. Those who have served only themselves will go into eternal punishment.

Sometimes we may be serving God in ways that we don't realize—by sharing a moment of time, cheering someone up, or by offering to help out our parents when they are busy.

People who do these chores often don't realize what they have done. They had a gift that they decided to use to help God. God gives us all gifts in order for us to share by helping others.   TLM

A Special Ministry (Friday)

"When did we see you sick or in prison and go to visit you?" (Matt. 25:39).

Recently, when our pastor went on vacation, the guest pastor was one who had a congregation at a local prison.

His sermon was different from most. He talked about his congregation and about the men his wife and he had met there. He invited anyone to join him there any Saturday night for the service and a fellowship hour afterward.

This man is bringing God to a place where men are starting their lives over and helping them start it off on the right foot.   TLM

Simple Acts of Kindness (Saturday)

"The righteous [will go] to eternal life" (Matt. 25:46).

When he comes again, the Lord will judge us all. The book of Matthew says that the evil "will go away to eternal punishment, but the righteous to eternal life."

We are told that by helping those less fortunate than ourselves we are helping the Lord.

When we visit a sick friend, feed a hungry person, or send clothes to a relief agency, we are helping the Lord. These simple acts of kindness which we show to each other are marks of our faith in Christ—faith that will lead to eternal life for us in the kingdom of the Lord.

TLM

Week 49   Mark 1:1-8

John the Baptist (Sunday)

John the Baptist didn't look particularly jolly. In fact, he would scare nearly any kid out of his wits. His hair was 30 years long, never been cut. He wore a super-rough, gunny-sack-like shirt. And if you joined him for lunch, he might offer you a honey-dipped grasshopper.

He preached a hard line, too. He knew Jesus was right behind him, so he wanted people to be ready. His message was urgent. "Repent and be baptized," he shouted. Many did. Many were. John put hard words and soft water together into an important religious experience. He made them feel sin-filthy with his preaching, and then he washed them squeaky clean in the Jordan River. He paved the way for Jesus by creating a congregation for him.

Many of the first followers of Jesus were even earlier followers of John the Baptist. He washed them clean—especially in the ears, so they could hear the words of Jesus.

Maybe some of us need to be sat down on a hillside and preached at with some tough words. Maybe we need to have God's word-sword cut deeply into us so we will first see our need for a Savior, and then see the Savior that we need in Jesus of Nazareth.

Even after 2000 years John helps us see that need and that Savior. John is still the waymaker, the tough-talking trailblazer of the church, and that's why we turn to him again and again, especially in the season of Advent, when we again prepare for the Christ child, the Christ man, the Christ God who is coming into the world.   SS

Teachers (Monday)

"I will send my messenger ahead of you, who will prepare your way" (Mark 1:2).

If it weren't for teachers, where would today's human society be? Not in the computer age, that's for sure. Teachers have a very important role in our society. They help prepare us for what we will face in the future. Whether the preparation is for a band concert at school or for a potential occupation, the intent is the same.

John the Baptist served the role of a teacher when he informed his "students" of the coming of Christ. He helped prepare them by baptizing them and preaching God's Word. Even now, it is up to us as students to put our preparation to work by teaching others, so they may be prepared too.   JAB

The Boy Scout Motto (Tuesday)

"Prepare the way for the Lord, make straight his paths for him" (Mark 1:3).

When I was in Boy Scouts, our motto was "Be prepared." Now whether it was to know what to do if you were lost in the woods without food or when to escort an elderly lady across the street, the motto encouraged us to be prepared.

As Christians we have the same motto and should take the same initiative. We all should prepare for Christ's second coming. That means devoting our entire life to him. We then will be able to help others to "Be prepared," so hopefully everyone will know the love of Christ.   JAB

A Life-style of Serving God (Wednesday)

"John wore clothing made of camel's hair, . . . and he ate locusts and wild honey" (Mark 1:6).

How would you like to take on a whole new life-style by giving up all your possessions, taking off for the desert, and surviving on bugs and honey? It doesn't sound too thrilling to me, but that is what John the Baptist did. He gave up a "normal" life so he could serve God.

Even though John lived 2000 years ago, we Christians should follow his example. I'm not saying that we all should pack up and head for the wilderness, but we can go out of our way and help spread God's Word in our own community. It isn't an easy job, but to see the joy of Christ growing in others is worth the sacrifice.   JAB

Diary of a Humble Man (Thursday)

"After me will come one more powerful than I, the thongs of whose sandals I am not worthy to stoop down and untie" (Mark 1:7).

There once was a man
  who was born in a dusty stable,
  who slept in a manger, because he had no crib,
  who grew up the son of a not-so-wealthy carpenter,
  who never had a high salary job,
  and who, despite all his humbleness,
  grew to be the King of all kings;
  yet still set enough time aside
  to love and appreciate
  each and every one of us.
He is
  Jesus Christ.   JAB

What Does It Mean? (Friday)

"He will baptize you with the Holy Spirit" (Mark 1:8).

"He will baptize you with the Holy Spirit." What does this mean? It is easy to understand how someone could baptize with water—but with the Holy Spirit? That is a little more difficult to comprehend.

What John the Baptist was saying as he stood in the River Jordan was that Christ would be coming to tell about the power of the Holy Spirit to all of us. So, as a result, we may know the true love of God the Father, God the Son, and God the Holy Spirit.   JAB

God's Breath (Saturday)

"He will baptize you with the Holy Spirit" (Mark 1:8).

During a windy Sunday afternoon in March, I set out to fly my kite. As my imitation bird soared hundreds of feet above my head, a little boy watched in awe. The next day I set out to fly my kite again, but this time there was no wind. Once again the little boy watched, only this time in bewilderment. He didn't know that I needed wind to fly my kite.

If God the Father, Son, and Holy Spirit were not working in our lives, we would be as useless as my kite was without any wind. But God breathes his Spirit ("breath" in the Old Testament) into us and gives us the power we need to live as Christians in the world.   JAB

Week 50 Psalm 43
Thirsting for God (Sunday)

So many of the psalms express the poet's longing to be
united with God or to know God more closely. That's
one reason many people turn to the Psalms. They put
into words our human longing. We wait and anticipate
the coming of God in power.

Waiting for childbirth is a universal experience.
Mothers and fathers wait for their children to be born.
They sometimes wait rather impatiently.

Occasionally a first-time mother is so excited about
being pregnant that she announces her condition very
early. As the long waiting period crawls along, her
friends begin to ask "When?" "How long?" It seems to
take forever. By her second or third child the same
woman won't tell anyone but her husband (and her
doctor) until the fourth or fifth month. Then they won't
needle her with their over-eager anticipations.

We formally anticipate Christ's birth in the church for
only a few weeks. We light candles in the church, and
we sometimes post calendars for our children, letting
them open little windows day-by-day, counting down the
time until Christmas.

The days before Christmas don't last long. They're
much shorter than the nine months that Mary and
Joseph had to wait. It is far, far shorter than the
hundreds and thousands of years the people of God
waited and prayed and longed. It is shorter than the
times the psalmists waited and prayed and longed and
sang. We all look for a time that we can draw near to
God, for a time that God will draw near us, for a time
that God will visit us, be with us, reveal himself to us.

Christmas is that time. It is a wonderful, blessed, holy
time. It is well worth waiting for.   SS

211

Rain (Monday)

"My soul thirsts for God, for the living God" (Ps. 42:2).

I gave my plants the dark black ground
in a really nice garden spot.
They had plenty of food and sunlight galore,
but water they had not.

Plants die, of course, from too much sun;
they lacked the falling rain.
Plants need the water to make them grow—
and turn seedlings into grain.

The same is true of Christian friends.
Too much sunshine dries us out,
so God sends rain to help us grow.
Believe it; do not doubt.   KK

Help (Tuesday)

"I will yet praise him, my Savior and my God" (Ps. 42:5)

I wish I knew why there must be
so many things inside of me
that turn my feelings inside out
and faithfulness back into doubt.

It all spins loosely in my mind,
not well thought out or well defined,
but there to make me question him
when chance for answers seems so slim

I guess I know they'll someday come
without much fuss or beat of drum,
when quiet voice inside my heart
says, "I've been helping from the start."   KK

God, Are You Listening? (Wednesday)

"At night his song is with me, a prayer to the God of my life" (Ps. 42:8).

God, are you listening?

It's been a lousy day, you know? My history teacher wants a 12-page paper on some guy I've never heard of. My mom is preparing me for a career as a garbage collector. (How can one family produce so much junk in a day?) And I've lost what's-her-name's class ring. I feel like I need time off from life.

God, I know you've got big things on your mind, but thanks for letting me sound off. Sometimes just knowing you care makes all the difference.   KK

Forgotten? (Thursday)

"I say to God, my Rock: 'Why have you forgotten me?' " (Ps. 42:9).

God always remembers to love us
and never forgets to forgive.
When the going gets tough and we're wondering how,
he shows us how to live.

God always remembers a kindness
and never forgets to be near.
When his children are struggling wildly,
he releases them from fear.

God always remembers a promise
and never forgets to be true.
These gifts he gives to all people.
He has not forgotten you.   KK

Giving In (Friday)

"Why must I go about mourning, oppressed by the enemy?" (Ps. 42:9).

Why am I always giving in, Lord?
    I let Jackie use the car again last weekend.
    I've done dinner dishes four nights in a row.
    I picked up the house before mom got home.
I'm sick of this, Lord.
    They all take me for granted.
    They know I'll do it.
I can't yell; it never gets me anywhere.
I can't not do things; they won't get done.
    Maybe I should give in again—
    to you though, not them.
Maybe you can handle them better than I can.   KK

Remembering (Saturday)

"Put your hope in God, for I will yet praise him" (Ps. 42:11).

I must remember:
though the sun may set
and the night is long,
the sun will rise again.
    I must remember:
    though the rain may fall
    and perhaps flood my life,
    it will dry again.
I must remember:
though God is distant to me,
and he might even seem lost,
I will find him again.
    Because I have already been found.   KK

Week 51 Luke 1:5-66
Mothers Young and Old (Sunday)

Elizabeth was almost too old to have a baby. But God arranged it. He sent the angel Gabriel into the temple while Zechariah was working there. Zechariah had a tough time believing the angel's announcement. His reward for second-guessing an angel was this: for the next nine months he was changed from a man of few words to a man of *no* words.

So the birth of John the Baptist was foretold. Elizabeth did conceive, and it all began to happen as predicted. Old Elizabeth felt the baby growing inside her.

Meanwhile, down in Nazareth, Gabriel also visited Mary. Hers was to be an even more startling story. Gabriel told her of Elizabeth's pregnancy, and that she too would conceive—but her baby would require no human father. Mary, bless her heart, had no trouble believing this (she was very young). Things began to happen inside her as well.

These two women later met at Zechariah's house in the hill country. Elizabeth was six months along, Mary just beginning her pregnancy. Elizabeth was almost too old for childbirth, Mary was scarcely old enough. When they met, John gave a great leap inside Elizabeth's womb. They took it as a sign.

So began the lives of two men who would change the world. John would prepare the way for Jesus, would baptize him, then transfer to Jesus his own followers. John would fade into obscurity and a premature death.

It all began with two faithful women and their husbands. Two generations met: old Elizabeth and young Mary. Two babies were born. The world will never be the same.   SS

God Hears Our Prayers (Monday)

"But the angel said to him:. . . 'Your prayer has been heard' " (Luke 1:13).

"Please, Lord," Tracy prayed, "I would like a boyfriend." But despite nightly prayers and months of waiting, no one asked Tracy out. "Aren't you listening, Lord?" Tracy felt as if she were just talking to herself.

But God *did* hear her prayers, as he hears every prayer of ours. We pray for what we *think* we want or need, but God *knows* what we need. Perhaps Tracy wasn't ready for the pressures and heartaches that come with having a boyfriend.

God knows (more than we do ourselves) what is best for us. He listens to our prayers and answers them in his time and way. Maybe God was saying to Tracy, "Not yet, Tracy, but be patient."   JS

Let Your Light Shine (Tuesday)

"Many of the people of Israel will he bring back to the Lord their God" (Luke 1:16).

Living in the wilderness, yelling "Repent!" and baptizing people in a river worked great for John the Baptist, but that isn't the only way to turn people to God.

As Christians, we want to share with others the inner peace we've found. Some well-meaning Christians who try to bring others to Christ are judgmental, narrowminded, and have an "I'm better than you are" attitude. Other Christians show unconditional patience and love. God continually refreshes them, and their contentment seems to radiate from them. People who have not found Christ sense this happiness and want to have it themselves.

Let us lead—not push—others to Christ.   JS

Always Be Prepared (Wednesday)

"He will. . . make ready a people prepared for the Lord" (Luke 1:17).

Mr. Carlson gave his students a pop quiz to see if they were keeping up with their assignments. The students who prepared for class daily did well; those who had not done the assignments did poorly.

The same is true of our relationship with God. We will face Christ when we least expect to. Those who prepare for him daily do not risk failing the biggest pop quiz of all—judgment day.

Let us believe in Christ, ask for forgiveness, and try to live a Christian life every day so that we are not unprepared for our death or for his second coming.   JS

Miracles (Thursday)

"For nothing is impossible with God" (Luke 1:37).

When we read the verse above we sometimes think, "That may have been true in the past, but what miracles does God perform *now?*"

God is not concerned with putting on a magician's show. God created nature and humans and uses them to do his will. We attribute the success of an operation to the doctor, but God was working *through* the doctor. We avoid an accident and say we were "lucky," but God was watching over us. We say rain and the sunshine make plants grow, but God created rain and sunshine. We are loved by another human, but God enables that person to love us. Miracles take place all around us, if only we do not let our senses grow too dull to notice.   JS

God's Standards Are Different (Friday)

"He has brought rulers down from their thrones but has lifted up the humble" (Luke 1:52).

Craig didn't make the basketball team, and he lost the student council election. He felt like everyone was better than he was.

In God's eyes Craig was not inferior. God does not shun the losers or those who are on the lowest end of society's scale. God chose a lower-class girl—not a queen—to bear his Son, Jesus. And Jesus himself talked to and cared about prostitutes and lepers.

When we feel as if no one wants to be our friend, and that others are better-looking, smarter, and more popular, we should remember that these things are insignificant to God. We are important and special to God.   JS

Happiness Cannot Be Bought (Saturday)

". . . The rich he has sent empty away" (Luke 1:53).

Mike always wanted more. His parents bought him a car, an expensive stereo, a camera, and a rifle, but Mike was never satisfied. Now he was begging his parents for a waterbed and a car stereo.

Mike had an empty, lonely place inside him which he thought he could fill with material possessions. He thought, "The more I have, the happier I'll be." But even though he was receiving many things, he was not getting any happier.

Mike's empty feeling could be filled only by Christ. And Christ teaches us that it is better to give than to receive. Giving—not getting—brings us satisfaction and true happiness.   JS

Week 52   Luke 2:1-20
Christmas (Sunday)

The birth of a baby can mean many things. It can be all joy. A set of parents who thought they would never have a child suddenly have one—like Sarah and Abraham, like Elizabeth and Zechariah.

It can be a mixed joy. A mother gives birth to a child whose father has been killed in a war or in an accident. The child is all the more precious to her because it is all she has left of her husband.

It can be a financial concern. A mother lives on welfare. There is precious little left for the three children she already has. How will this child affect them all?

It can be anger and guilt and shame. The girl has bravely refused to abort her baby. She has lived in a special prenatal home and will give her baby up for adoption. Her parents don't understand. They never will. The baby has just made their differences more obvious.

It can be the answer to hopes and prayers. A couple who could never have a child of their own will take that baby, given up for adoption, and raise it as their own.

It can be a baby the whole world waits for, a baby predicted by prophets since ancient times, a baby whose conception and whose birth was heralded by angels, a baby whose very existence will threaten thrones and cause plottings in high places, a baby whose life and growth will be monitored by God himself.

Such a baby we receive on Christmas Eve. Such a child begins his days on Christmas Day. His adulthood will revive all possible reactions to birth and life—joy, concern, anger, guilt, shame, hope, and answer to prayer.

The birth of Jesus changes things, even the condition of your birth and mine. How is your life being changed by the birth of Jesus?   SS

What's God Doing There? (Monday)

"And she gave birth to her firstborn, a son" (Luke 2:7).

What's God doing there, in a baby, in a man? Such tiny hands and feet! I've never seen such a calm little baby. He must know that God is in him and that he need not cry.

Today a lamb is born in Bethlehem, a lamb without a blemish, a right and clean sacrifice to our God. Just wait until the lamb grows. Then be sharp, knife! Then be ready, priests!

"See how much I love you?" says God. "This much. Now wipe dry your tears. Let's dance! I'll teach you. My son, who is Christ the Lord, is born! I love you, children! Dance!"
PAF

Greatness (Tuesday)

"She wrapped him in cloths and placed him in a manger" (Luke 2:7).

Here. This is greatness: a stable. You've had it all wrong since Eden. I've come now to change this world, to refresh your memories, to show you the lie you've believed for so long.

So I don't do things your way. I'm born in a stable, not a palace; greeted by shepherds, not Pharisees; my mother unwed, not a respectable queen. But my father is God; that makes all the difference. I shall feed the hungry, heal the sick, touch lepers, eat with sinners, die a criminal's death. See, *that* is greatness: God coming to the bottom. I cannot save you any other way. If you love me, follow me.
PAF

Evangelists (Wednesday)

"I bring you good news of great joy that will be for all the people" (Luke 2:10).

"The Messiah is come," said the angel, and Jesus' first evangelists were made—eager, stumbling shepherds, frightened and amazed. "We can't be quiet about this! Our *Messiah!* Here! Now! Praise the God of Israel!" They went running through the night: "We've seen the Messiah!"

"A great joy that will be for *all* the people," the angel said. This was its start.

I haven't seen the Messiah face to face, but I have the Bible, full of stories about him, and I have my own life and stories of my own. Who am I to stay quiet and still? Our Messiah is come! Let all the people know!   PAF

All That's Left of David (Thursday)

"And all who heard it were amazed at what the shepherds said to them" (Luke 2:18).

What on earth would the Messiah be doing in a manger? He's supposed to be descended from David—a king, not a carpenter's son. What happened to David's line anyway? Wasn't it to continue forever? A Gentile claims to be our ruler now. The shepherds did say the baby's father was of David. Is this all that's left of David? Is Israel so low that our Messiah is a poor man's son?

Actually, even King David started out low. He was his father's youngest son and a shepherd, but he was the greatest king Israel ever had. What will God do with this baby who doesn't even have a proper bed? Something greater than David!   PAF

Glory (Friday)

"But Mary treasured up all these things and pondered them in her heart" (Luke 2:19).

Mary—
unmarried,
engaged,
but not wife.
Yet
she cradles her son.
He's not Joseph's son,
but the one called Son of the Most High.
A lot to think about—
angels and shepherds, and the Messiah in her lap.
Bow your head, too, and join her.
Ponder once more
the glory of God!   PAF

Joy (Saturday)

"And the shepherds returned, glorifying and praising God for all the things they had heard and seen, which were just as they had been told" (Luke 2:20).

The Christmas carols are so old. Oh, I've found that they can be wonderful if you listen hard (my favorite is "What Child Is This?"), but I'd like some new ones. Ones with trumpets (at least 17 of them), ones with dancing, ones with laughter. The greatest thing that could ever happen has happened!

Where's our joy? We determine the goodness of Christmas by the size of the pile of presents under the tree; we should determine it by the size of the joy in our hearts, the joy that makes us different people forever. For our God is great indeed!   PAF